# The Kindness of God

# The Kindness of God

*Metaphor, Gender, and Religious Language*

Janet Martin Soskice

**OXFORD**
UNIVERSITY PRESS

# OXFORD
UNIVERSITY PRESS

Great Clarendon Street, Oxford OX2 6DP

Oxford University Press is a department of the University of Oxford.
It furthers the University's objective of excellence in research, scholarship,
and education by publishing worldwide in

Oxford New York

Auckland Cape Town Dar es Salaam Hong Kong Karachi
Kuala Lumpur Madrid Melbourne Mexico City Nairobi
New Delhi Shanghai Taipei Toronto

With offices in

Argentina Austria Brazil Chile Czech Republic France Greece
Guatemala Hungary Italy Japan Poland Portugal Singapore
South Korea Switzerland Thailand Turkey Ukraine Vietnam

Oxford is a registered trade mark of Oxford University Press
in the UK and in certain other countries

Published in the United States
by Oxford University Press Inc., New York

British Library Cataloguing in Publication Data

Data available

Library of Congress Cataloging in Publication Data

Data available

Typeset by SPI Publisher Services, Pondicherry, India
Printed in Great Britain
on acid-free paper by
Clays Ltd., St Ives plc

ISBN 978–0–19–826951–9 (Hbk.)
978–0–19–826950–2 (Pbk.)

1

*I dedicate this book to Effie Hunter who, at 97, has waited long enough to see it, but lived the reality all her life.*

# Acknowledgements

I have received encouragement and advice from many friends in the course of writing the essays that make up this book. I would here like especially to thank Gillian Price, who, with great patience as my editorial assistant, helped me see it to press. In its early stages I was the beneficiary of a Canada Commonwealth Fellowship at the Centre for Studies in Religion and Society in the University of Victoria, and I must thank friends and colleagues there, and especially Harold Coward, the former and founding Director of the Centre.

Portions of this book have been previously published in earlier versions as follows: Chapter 1, 'Love and Attention', in Michael McGhee (ed.), *Philosophy, Religion and Spiritual Life* (Cambridge: Cambridge University Press, 1992); Chapter 2, 'Imago Dei', in *Concilium*, 2006/1; Chapter 3, 'Creation and Relation', in *Theology*, Jan.–Feb. 1991; Chapter 4, 'Can a Feminist Call God "Father"?', in Alvin Kimel (ed.), *Speaking the Christian God: The Holy Trinity and the Challenge of Feminism* (Grand Rapids, MI: Eerdmans, 1992) and also in Teresa Elwes, *Women's Voices in Religion: Essays in Contemporary Feminist Theology* (London: Collins, 1992); Chapter 5, 'Blood and Defilement', in *ET: Journal of the European Society for Catholic Theology*,

# Acknowledgements

2 (Tübingen, 1994); Chapter 6, 'Trinity and the "Feminine Other"', *New Blackfriars*, Jan. 1994; and Chapter 8, 'Friendship', in Marco M. Olivetti (ed.), *Intersubjectivité et Théologie Philosophique*, Proceedings of the Castelli Colloquium (Rome: Cedam, 2001).

# Contents

Introduction                                                                  1

1.  Love and Attention: Incarnateness                                         7

2.  *Imago Dei*                                                              35

3.  Creation and Relation                                                    52

4.  Calling God 'Father'                                                      66

5.  Blood and Defilement: Christology                                        84

6.  Trinity and the 'Feminine Other'                                        100

7.  The Kindness of God: Trinity and
    the Image of God in Julian of
    Norwich and Augustine                                                   125

8.  Friendship: love thy neighbour                                          157

9.  Being Lovely: Eschatological
    Anthropology                                                            181

Bibliography                                                                189

Index                                                                       199

# Introduction

THERE are many metaphorical names for God in the biblical literature—Rock, Shepherd, Lamb, Fortress, Door, Way—but playing a privileged role amongst them are anthropomorphic titles. These personify God, and it seems that the biblical writers were pressed to use anthropomorphism to do justice to a God whose acts they wished to chronicle. This is a God who cajoles, chastises, soothes, alarms, and loves, and in our experience it is human beings who pre-eminently do these things. Early Christian theologians saw in this plenitude of divine titles a revelation of the manner in which God, while remaining one and holy mystery, is in diverse ways 'God *with us*'.

We can identify biblical anthropomorphic titles in three registers: those appropriate to offices of governance, for instance, where God is Lord, King, and Judge; those related to offices of service, in which God is Shepherd, Watchman, or Servant (Teacher might fall into either of these two categories); and those representing the offices of love—Father, Brother, Son, Spouse, Lover. These last are the most intimate, because they are all, if we extend some generosity to Spouse and Lover, kinship titles.

# Introduction

Kinship imagery is both compelled and resisted by the Hebrew scriptures, compelled for reasons of intimacy, and resisted from fear of idolatry. Thus the remarkable 'Song of Moses' at the end of Deuteronomy not only provides one of the few instances of naming God 'Father' in the Old Testament ('Is he not your father, who created you, who made and established you?' (Deut. 32: 6)),[1] but goes on to follow this with a graphic maternal image, accusing Israel of being 'unmindful of the Rock that bore you' and forgetting 'the God who gave you birth'. Paternal and maternal imagery in quick succession effectively rules out literalism, as does the astonishing invocation of a parturient rock. The text both gives and takes away, for it is on the face of it preposterous that we, creatures, should be the kin of God.

Yet there is a sense in which both Old and New Testaments point to nothing less. Kinship titles are mutually implying—if I am your kin, then you are mine. Once one has a brother or a sister, one *is* a brother or a sister. This is not merely a matter of emotional and domestic ties. A shepherd who ceases to look after sheep is no longer a shepherd. He might become a farmer or, as in David's case, a king. Kinship terms are not similarly disposable. A woman who gives birth is made a mother by the arrival of the child, and this is so, formally, even if the child is taken away without her seeing it, or dies within a few days of birth. The relation of mother to child is formal as well as, in most cases, emotional. To claim that God is our Father, or Christ our brother, is thus to make a strong claim not only about God but about us.

---

[1] Biblical quotations are from the NRSV.

2

# Introduction

Given this strength of implication, we should be more startled than we are by the kinship titles in the Bible. Yet for many centuries and until relatively recently, kinship titles and related imagery (father, brother, being 'born again') was little remarked background noise of Christianity—the common and effaced coin of Christian speech (see Chapters 4, 5, and 7). Derrida wrote of a 'white mythology', referring to the ballast of dead metaphors (the 'stem' of a wine glass, a 'high' note, economic 'inflation') in ordinary language so pervasive as to pass unnoticed. Christian teaching, we could say, has been for many centuries in receipt of a 'grey mythology'—metaphors worn smooth, like an old marble staircase, through centuries of stately liturgical ascent until their original figurative potency was lost. It was left to a later day for kinship metaphors to disturb and scandalize, but also to reawaken us to the promise of what we may become.

This is effectively what happened in the early days of feminist theology. It is not that earlier generations had excluded the possibility that God might be called Mother as well as Father; it was simply in most cases not considered. It was not, however, possible for any theologian of my generation, or sex, and especially not one like me whose special interest lay in religious language, to ignore questions of gendered imagery. Here were questions not only deeply interesting in their own right but, unlike many that absorb the academy, ones which had the deepest bearing on the lives of individuals and of their churches. The initial response to these genuine difficulties was, in some cases, to try to excise 'sexed' titles, a project which proved difficult with liturgy and impossible with Scripture. When we change the gender of a term, often as not we change the relationship: a child in general does not occupy the

3

# Introduction

same status in biblical literature as the first-born son.[2] While this seems to put us between a rock and a hard place (either give up the Bible or embrace its outmoded categories), the idea that the biblical books, or parts of them, are too intrinsically sexist to be sustaining for modern readers betrays a strangely wooden literary theory. Books do not contain their contents with the fixity that an individual volume contains so many grams of paper and so many of printer's ink. The message of a book cannot be separated from its living readership, a point made by many modern literary theorists, but long realized by rabbis and theologians who distinguished between the inspiration of Scripture and the illumination of those individuals and communities who read them.

Many of the essays in this volume had their origins in a desire to explore the symbolics of sex and in my attendant conviction that if feminism was to be of enduring importance to theology, it must result in constructive as well as critical work. My plan was, in exploring the gendered imagery, to move the reader through many of the main loci of Christian reflection—the nature of God and creation, Christian anthropology, Christology, Trinity. I hope the volume still works in this way. But as the work proceeded, and especially as I explored the systematic connections, it seemed more and more evident that the principal reason why the biblical writings are so dependent on gendered imagery (a dependence which increases as we move from the Old Testament to the New) is not because its writers were so very interested in sex, or even hierarchy and subordination, but because they were interested in kinship.

[2] On this see my essay, 'The Symbolics of Staying On', in D. Hampson (ed.), *Swallowing the Fishbone: Christian and Post-Christian Feminism* (London: SPCK, 1996), 17–32.

# Introduction

In Middle English the words 'kind' and 'kin' were the same—to say that Christ is 'our kinde Lord' is not to say that Christ is tender and gentle, although that may be implied, but to say that he is kin—our kind. This fact, and not emotional disposition, is the rock which is our salvation. The title of this book wants to recapture that association.

Kinship may seem, in our egalitarian times, to be a dangerous theological direction to go in not least if we associate kinship titles with dominance and subordination. Without doubt, kinship terms have been used to enforce a certain rigidity into Christian anthropology (what used to be called the 'Christian Doctrine of Man'), but my wager is that if we return to the texts of Scripture and the classical texts of theology, many of these fears will be dispelled. In Matthew's gospel Jesus exploded normal expectations by asking, 'Who is my mother, and who are my brothers?' (Matt. 12: 48). Early Christians scandalized late antique society by eschewing marriage and choosing to belong as celibates to a new family of brothers and sisters in Christ. The hierarchical expectations of fatherhood and sonship were up-ended by the formulations of the doctrine of the Trinity (Chapter 6).

Undoubtedly this spirit of freedom in the anthropology of the early fathers was constrained by the particular notions of human perfection with which they worked. Abetted by the Hellenism which was the air they breathed, many early theologians reached a picture of the perfect Christian whose contemplative stillness mirrored that of the impassible Deity (Chapters 1, 2, and 7). This is a far cry from the representation of the human condition in the Bible, which is perfected not in solitary changelessness but in its special mixture of holiness, fractious indignity, and other people, including mothers, fathers, brothers, and lovers (Chapters 1, 2, 6, 7, and 8).

Kinship imagery has this signal advantage—it is all about birth, growth, and change. From their first appearance in the Old Testament, the divine kinship titles are names of promise, holding before us the vision of a love which is both now and not yet. The family of God is both now and yet to come, and what we will be—either individually or collectively—is not yet apparent. Metaphors of kinship open up for us an eschatological anthropology wherein our constant becoming is our way of being children of God. It is with these themes of birth, growth, and change that these essays begin.

# 1

# Love and Attention

## I

The matched pair 'love' and 'attention' form the pivot of the essays in Iris Murdoch's philosophical classic *Sovereignty of the Good*. Although Murdoch tells us in that book that there is, in her view, no God in the traditional sense of that term, she provides accounts of art, prayer, and morality that are religious; for morality 'has always been connected with religion and religion with mysticism'.[1] The connection here is love and attention: art and morals are two aspects of the same struggle; both involve attending, a task of attention which goes on all the time, efforts of imagination which are important cumulatively. 'Virtue is *au fond* the same in the artist as in the good man in that it is a selfless attention to nature.' 'Prayer', says this most religious of agnostics, 'is properly not petition, but simply an attention to God which is a form of love.'[2]

Murdoch acknowledges her debt to Simone Weil, and the writings of both have, in turn, influenced many others—including Charles Taylor. For Taylor, too, moral and spiritual intuitions go together. Orientation to the good is not an optional aspect

---

[1] I. Murdoch, *The Sovereignty of Good* (London: Routledge Classics, 2001), 74.
[2] Ibid. 41, 55.

7

of human being that may be engaged in or abstained from at will, but a condition of our being 'selves with an identity'.[3] All of us are directed by our loves and desires, but we must ask *what* we love, *what* we attend to, in order to know *who we are and should be*.

So it seems that 'love' and 'attention' provide a meeting point for philosophy, religion, and the spiritual life, with the further desirable feature that the ethical is central to the meeting. Love on this reading is a central concept in morals. To be fully human and moral is to respond to that which demands or compels our response—the other attended to with love. It is this loving which both draws us out of ourselves and constitutes us fully as selves. For Murdoch the best exemplar of the 'unselfish' by attention is our experience of beauty: 'I am looking out of my window in an anxious and resentful state of mind . . . suddenly I observe a hovering kestrel. In a moment everything is altered. The brooding self with its hurt vanity has disappeared. There is now nothing but kestrel.'[4]

We respond to the 'Good' or the 'Beautiful'. There is a debt to Plato in this idea of a Good, the love of which enables us to do good and be good. It opens up a view of the good life which 'takes us far beyond the purview of the morals of obligatory action' with which much modern mainstream moral theory has contented itself.[5] We would normally be far from thinking that ethics is a matter of 'seeing' and of loving, or that our ethical life is linked with our love for the order of the world around us and our attending to its exact particularity, whether

[3] C. Taylor, *Sources of the Self: The Making of the Modern Identity* (Cambridge: Cambridge University Press, 1989), 68.

[4] Murdoch, *Sovereignty of Good*, 84.

[5] Taylor, *Sources of the Self*, 93.

to the flight of the kestrel, the unfurling of a peony, or the course of the planets. In this we differ from the ancients.

In ancient philosophy, both Platonic and Aristotelian, practical wisdom, the kind employed in the moral life, involved *seeing* an order already given in nature. This was because the Divine might be glimpsed behind the things of this world—each particular was a trace, a hint, a lead, to that which was both supremely desirable and supremely intelligible. Although neither Plato nor Aristotle embraced the notion of a 'personal' God, they had a religious metaphysic. Aristotle's studies of plants and animals, even of the 'contemptible' ones, were not driven by idle curiosity or a bald empiricism. He believed that we can find in all the works of Nature 'something wonderful', because we can sense in them the divine presence. We delight in the stars or the starfish because 'we find in them, directly or indirectly, a trace of that reality which attracts us irresistibly', the First Principle which, Aristotle believed 'moves all things as the beloved moves the lover'.[6]

Because it is given and real and holy, the world calls for our attention, which Murdoch defines as 'a just and loving gaze directed upon an individual reality'. Attention is, she says, the 'characteristic and proper mark of the active moral agent'.[7] Attentive love is close to contemplation.

How differently we see the reasoning and the moral agent now. Even in Christian ethics the moral agent is more likely to be portrayed as one executing a delicate calculus of moral gains and losses before pursuing a particular course of action, than as one attentive to the beauty and harmony of creation. Descartes,

---

[6] P. Hadot, *What is Ancient Philosophy?* (Cambridge, Mass., and London: Belknap Press of Harvard University Press, 2004), 84.

[7] Murdoch, *Sovereignty of Good*, 34.

philosophizing in his stove, mentally divested himself of his body and the world. In his search for certainty he concluded that no knowledge comes from gazing at the beauty and harmony of creation; vision is not a key to the divine but, rather, like all the senses, liable to deceive. The 'I' can only find certainty by first doubting everything it sees, everything it knows— the very world—before settling on the certainty of the thinking self.[8] But the cost is high. The man of reason gains certainty by distancing himself from that which is known. Even our own bodies become snares and mysteries to this worldless 'cogito'. We still cannot be rid of the idea, especially when we are doing philosophy, that we are brains on sticks.

Neither Iris Murdoch nor Charles Taylor have much time for the 'man of reason' who in various guises trudges through the works of early modern philosophy, a disengaged self in the disenchanted universe. Here is Murdoch's description of Rational Man:

How recognisable, how familiar to us, is the man so beautifully portrayed in the *Grundlegung*, who confronted even with Christ turns away to consider the judgement of his own conscience and to hear the voice of his own reason...this man is with us still, free, independent, lonely, powerful, rational, responsible, brave, the hero of so many novels and books of moral philosophy... He is the offspring of the age of science, confidently rational and yet increasingly aware of his alienation from the material universe which his discoveries reveal.[9]

---

[8] This is not, of course, an answer to doubt so much as a starting point for rebuilding knowledge in Descartes's scheme, for we could still ask, 'what subtends thought?' Modern empiricism takes nothing for granted. The world it studies and observes, often to great and productive effect, is, from the point of view of modern science, a brute reality. To say more is to speculate. Materialism, the view that there is 'nothing but' matter, is also a metaphysical position, and speculative, rather than a matter of scientific fact, as its proponents suggest.

[9] Murdoch, *Sovereignty of Good*, 80.

This is he who is 'capable of objectifying not only the surrounding world but also his own emotions and inclinations, fears and compulsions, and achieving thereby a kind of distance and self-possession which allows him to act "rationally"'.[10]

This new agent of science gains control, even in his moral life, through 'disengagement' and objectification. Radical subjectivity made the new radical objectivity possible. The Cartesian turn to the self, which entails a turn from the other, is a requirement of a philosophy that will subsequently break down into the indubitable 'in here' and the unreliable 'out there', a philosophy in which it becomes not only possible but necessary to regard the rest of the world as objects, distant and no part of me. Once confined securely within our selves, we can manipulate and control a world of objects.[11] Even our affective responses come to have a value analogous in early modern philosophy and science to secondary properties such as 'red' and 'pain'.[12] If God is to be found at all—and Descartes was a Christian—then God will be found through the self and the soul, and not through the world around us or even other people. Like most heresies, this one is a good theological tenet gone out of control—in this case the idea that to be in *imago Dei* (construed as participating in divine rationality) means in some sense, epistemologically, to be God. It is curious that Christianity, whose central doctrine is the Incarnation, could be used to underwrite an epistemological programme in which man attempts to distance himself from the human condition.

---

[10] Taylor, *Sources of the Self*, 21.

[11] Ibid. 173–4.

[12] Accurate knowledge requires us to 'suspend the "intentional" dimension of experience, that is, what makes it an experience *of* something' (ibid. 162).

Many have drawn attention to the Augustinian ancestry of this modern disengaged self and its radical reflexivity, but Augustine's self-doubt was different from that of Descartes, as was his final certainty. Augustine's doubting ended, not when he was certain he existed because he could not doubt that he was thinking, but with the acknowledgement that, although he did not know himself, he knew that he was known by God. Augustine's broader anthropology depends at every point on his understanding that creation itself, and his own being within it, is always already a gift, and he thus avoids the Promethean self-positing of Descartes's *Meditations*. Nonetheless, Augustine and many other Christian fathers prized a detachment from circumstances, distractions, and even the body itself which anticipates the privacy and self-mastery of the 'Man of Reason'. Indeed, this ideal of self-mastery is a familiar figure in modern texts of spiritual theology. Despite the criticisms which the 'disengaged self' or 'Rational Man' has received in recent years from philosophers, his theological near-relation, 'Spiritual Man', has continued virtually unchallenged, especially in what might be called 'received spirituality'.

## II

For many people the phrase 'the spiritual life' conjures up something still and luminous, turned to the future and far from our daily lives, where, spiritually, we just 'bump along'. I believe we can also speak of a 'received view' of spiritual life as involving long periods of quiet, focused reflection, dark churches, and dignified liturgies. In its higher reaches it involves time spent

# Love and Attention

in contemplative prayer, retreats, and sometimes the painful
wrestlings with God portrayed by John Donne or George Her-
bert. Above all, it involves solitude and collectedness. It does
not involve looking after small children.

In the past I have been envious and in awe of colleagues
(usually bachelors) who spend their holidays living with monks
in the Egyptian desert or making long retreats on Mount
Athos. They return refreshed and renewed, and say such things
as 'It was wonderful. I was able to reread the whole of *The City
of God* in the Latin ... something I've not done for three or four
years now.' I recall my own holidays as entirely taken up with
explaining why you can't swim in the river with an infected ear,
why two ice-creams before lunch is a bad idea, with trips to
disgusting public conveniences with children who are 'desper-
ate', with washing grubby clothes, pouring cooling drinks, and
cooking meals in inconvenient kitchens for children made
cranky by too much sun and water. From such holidays one
returns exhausted and wondering why people go on holiday.
But family holidays are only memorable instances of a wider
whole. Parents of small children find themselves looking
enviously over the wall at their more spiritual brethren—are
these not the true 'spiritual athletes' whose disciplined life of
prayer brings them daily closer to God? The 'received view' of
the spiritual life seems to confirm this, as does a good deal of
guidance from priests and pastors. One story will have to
suffice. A devout Anglican woman of my acquaintance had
her first baby. Like most new mothers, she was exhausted, but
she was also distraught to find her devotional life in ruins. She
took advice from three priests. The first told her that if the baby
woke at 6.00 a.m., she should rise at 5.00 a.m. for a quiet hour
of prayer. The second asked if her husband could not arrange to

13

come home early from work three times a week so that she could get to a Mass. This advice proved threatening to life and marriage. The third told her, 'Relax and just look after your baby. The rest of the Church is praying for you.'

The advice of the third was the best and shows, too, why one doesn't really resent the retreatant on Mount Athos or religious contemplatives. These people are praying for us all. But still the priest's advice is not entirely consoling. Is the busy new mother a sort of Christian 'on idle'? Will others carry on seeking God's face while you spend eight or ten or twelve years distracted by the cares of the home? Is this the 'Martha' phase of life when you run the crèche and make the tea, while the real work of attending to God is elsewhere? Not surprisingly, many new mothers feel slightly bitter about this state of affairs.

Despite markers that could lead elsewhere, Christian 'received spirituality' is still shaped by particular views of contemplative life and of what it is to be in the image of God that disenfranchise many people, and perhaps especially women.[13]

The 'received view' has a noble ancestry. Consider Gregory of Nyssa's influential treatise *On Virginity*, written sometime around 368 CE. It is not easy, says the author, to find quiet for divine contemplation within secular life, and as he would create in his readers a passion for excellence, he recommends as a 'necessary door of entrance to the holier life, the calling of Virginity'.[14] His praise of virginity takes an interesting tack.

---

[13] 'Received spirituality' is probably also a fantasy remote from the actual busy lives of many monks and nuns.

[14] Gregory of Nyssa, '*On Virginity*', in Gregory of Nyssa, *Select Works*, Nicene and Post-Nicene, Series 2, Vol. 5 (Grand Rapids, Mich.: Wm. B. Eerdmans Publishing Co., 1979), 343.

He does not, as might be expected by our prurient age, condemn sexual activity. Rather, he reserves his disapprobation for marriage, even for an 'ideal' marriage. Consider a marriage in every way most happy—illustrious birth, competent means, deep affection. Beneath these blessings 'the fire of an inevitable pain is smouldering'.[15] The young wife will grow old and die, she may on the other hand die young in childbirth, and the child with her. Children born safely may be subject to accident, illness, and disease. You (male) may die on a business trip. A young wife is soon a widow, friends desert her, families quarrel, finances fall to pieces. In short, family life is one damn thing after another. 'He whose life is contained in himself', says Gregory, can easily bear these things, 'possessing a collected mind which is not distracted from itself; while he who shares himself with wife and child' is totally taken up with anxiety for his dear ones.[16]

The striking thing about Gregory's analysis is that it is so convincing. He is simply right, and while we in the West may be spared many terrors of deaths in childbirth, we can list other vexations which erode time and energy and would take us from contemplative quiet in the way Gregory describes.

But what about the medicine he prescribes? There is only one way, he says, to escape from Nature's inevitable snares:

it is, to be attached to none of these things, and to get as far away as possible from the society of this emotional and sensual world; or rather, for *a man to go outside the feelings which his own body gives rise to*. Then, as he does not live for the flesh, he will not be subject to the troubles of the flesh.[17]

---

[15] Ibid. 345.    [16] Ibid. 347.
[17] Gregory of Nyssa, 'On Virginity', in Gregory of Nyssa, *Select Works*, Nicene and Post-Nicene, Series 2, Vol. 5 (Grand Rapids, Mich.: Wm. B. Eerdmans Publishing Co., 1979), 350–1, my italics.

He will not be disturbed then by the troubles of his own flesh, nor by the disturbing and demanding flesh of spouse and children. By this means, Gregory says, we may emulate the spirits who neither marry nor are given in marriage, but rather 'contemplate the Father of all purity'.

How can the soul which is riveted to the pleasures of the flesh and busied with *merely human longings* turn a disengaged eye upon its kindred intellectual light?...The eyes of swine, turning naturally downwards, have no glimpse of the wonders of the sky; no more can the soul whose body drags it down look anymore upon the beauty above; it must pore perforce upon things which though natural are low and animal. To look with a free devoted gaze upon heavenly delights, the soul...will transfer all its power of affection from material objects to the intellectual contemplation of immaterial beauty.[18]

Once freed, the soul in its virgin state can emulate the God who is pure, free, and changeless. Gregory takes seriously the idea that man is made in the image of God, but transposes from an idealized 'Man' a picture of God as sovereign, rational, and free, the very image of 'disengaged man'.

Early Christian ascetics fled the cities and sought the deserts of Egypt and Syria, convinced that the world would soon come to an end and informed by disciplines of self-mastery (*enkrateia*) they had adopted from the pagan philosophical schools. The most ascetic went to such extremes of self-denial in order to escape the body while remaining alive that they were considered heretical. Nonetheless, the spiritual disciplines of the philosophers were attractive to Christians for their assault on

---

[18] Ibid. 351, my italics.

egocentrism and advocacy of the contemplative life. Socrates in the *Phaedo* had advocated 'separating the soul as much as possible from the body'[19] in order to move from particular to universal, and then on to the world of pure thought. The *Enneads* of Plotinus, a third-century Neoplatonist work that influenced Augustine and many other Christian writers, sketched a pattern for spiritual growth in which the soul, once purified from attachments to the body and then the sensible world, seeks final, wordless union with the One. For the Stoics, distancing oneself as far as possible emotionally from concerns of the body, worries of the world, and ultimately, we might say, from other people was the way to a true happiness consisting of independence and freedom.[20] One should have no goal outside oneself, and then, being dependent on no one else for happiness, one cannot be made unhappy. The model for this self-sufficiency was the Divine. In Aristotle's system, 'God'—or 'Thought which thinks'—exists in eternal indifference to and inactivity towards the world, and 'has no object or goal other than itself'.[21]

Aristotle's God, eternally oblivious to the world, is a far cry from the God of Abraham and Isaac and Jacob, and escape from the body always fitted uneasily with Christianity, not only because of its earthy, Jewish roots, but because of its central teaching. This teaching, repellent to the philosophers of the ancient world, is that God became a man with a body like that of other men, the Word was made flesh, born of a woman and put to death on a cross. The body is

---

[19] Quoted by Hadot, *What is Ancient Philosophy?*, 94.

[20] A Stoic might be entirely engaged in affairs of the world, witness the Emperor Marcus Aurelius, while striving for this inner detachment. But it is this inner detachment which is, in terms of other people, the problem. If I am not unsettled by grief, have I ever known love?

[21] Quoted in Hadot, *What is Ancient Philosophy?*, 81.

central to all these divine activities. Jesus in his life, and even more in his death, showed little of the indifference to his body, his family, or his friends prized by the sages. Nevertheless, the Christian fathers had difficulty in affirming the body and its distractions, and preferred to embrace 'self-mastery' (*enkrateia*) as a route to 'unselving' and virginity as the ideal Christian way of life.

Even if we allow for rhetorical excess, it cannot be doubted that Gregory of Nyssa's *Treatise on Virginity* invokes a spiritual ideal in which the demands of others, even of one's own babies and children, are not merely indifferent to the task of gazing on God, but in competition with it. The higher life is akin to that of Plato; reason, defined in terms of a vision of order, purity, and immutability, governs desire. The 'good' man is 'master of himself'.[22]

A Latin counterpart to Gregory's essay may be found in the first book of *De Doctrina Christiana*, one of Augustine's early works. Here he develops a distinction between things which we are to enjoy and things which we are to use. That which we enjoy makes us happy, we take satisfaction in it for its own sake. Those things which are objects of our use, on the other hand, help move towards that which will make us happy. But should we set ourselves to 'enjoy' what should properly only be 'used', we are hindered on our way.

Augustine illustrates this with the simile of a voyage: suppose we were wanderers in a strange country and could not live happily away from home. Yet the beauty of the country through which we pass or the pleasure of travel may divert us from 'that home whose delights would make us truly happy.

[22] Taylor, *Sources of the Self*, 115.

Such is a picture of our condition of this life of mortality. We have wandered far from God; and if we wish to return to our Father's home, this world must be used, not enjoyed.'[23] It is our duty rather to 'enjoy the truth which lives unchangeably', for no one, according to Augustine, 'is so egregiously silly' as to doubt 'that a life of unchangeable wisdom is preferable to one of change'.[24] It is only the strength of evil habits that draws us to less valuable objects in preference to the more worthy. Human loves, as Augustine knew, bring bereavement and sorrow; 'those only are the true objects of enjoyment' which are 'eternal and unchangeable. The rest are for use.'[25] Even our neighbour, whom we are commanded to love, we love for the sake of something else—that is, in Augustine's terms, 'we use him'. The contrasts are between the eternal, changeless, and divine and the temporary and material. The latter—even one's own children—should only be used on our way to the former.

This harsh-sounding suggestion needs to be qualified. To love others properly is to love them as they are loved by God. Once we see other people as created and loved by God, they are returned to us as signs of the love which made them and which is their true end. Nonetheless, Augustine remains troubled, even in the *Confessions*, by the strength of his passions and his inability to control them. At his mother's deathbed he struggled with his grief, and only by what he calls a 'powerful act of mental control' held back the flood of tears, an inappropriate response since he knows that Monica's death did not

---

[23] Augustine, *On Christian Teaching*, ed. R. P. H. Green (Oxford: Oxford University Press, 1997), 523.
[24] Ibid. 525.
[25] Ibid. 527.

mean that 'her state was miserable, nor that she was suffering extinction'.[26] The new Christian is an old Stoic. His son, Adeodatus, is not so constrained, and his tears have to be checked. Augustine carries out his duties as a son, making arrangements for the funeral, sees the body carried out, and so on, without shedding a tear, so that those who listened to him intently, he says, 'supposed me to have no feeling of grief'. But inwardly he is troubled not only by overwhelming grief, as if his life 'were torn to pieces', but by puzzlement as to why he should suffer such grief—'it caused me sharp displeasure to see how much power these human frailties had over me, though they are a necessary part of the order we have to endure and are the lot of the human condition'—a twofold sadness. 'I could be reproached', he adds, 'for yielding to that emotion of physical kinship.'[27]

Few will be attracted or convinced by Augustine's account of 'enjoyment' and 'use' when it comes to other people, an account which even he may have regarded as 'experimental and finally inconclusive'.[28] Neither Gregory nor Augustine managed to stop Christians from marrying or forming attachments

---

[26] Augustine, *Confessions* (London: Hodder & Stoughton, 1997), IX. xiii. 29–33.

[27] Ibid. IX. xiii. 34. By the time of writing *The City of God*, a note of Christian realism is evident. Augustine notes that Jesus himself was angered, wept, and yearned to share the Passover meal with his disciples. We, however, sometimes yield to irrational emotions, as when we weep for those we know bound for heaven. 'Yet if we felt none of these emotions at all, while we are subject to the weakness of this life, there would really be something wrong with our life.' *Apatheia*, if that means freedom from emotions in defiance of reason which disturb our thoughts, is clearly a good thing, he says, but not one that belongs to the present life (*City of God*, XIV. 9, trans. Henry Bettenson (London: Penguin Classics, 1984)).

[28] O. O'Donovan, *The Problem of Self-Love in St. Augustine* (New Haven and London: Yale University Press, 1980), 26.

to mothers, fathers, brothers, sisters, husbands, wives, and children.[29] But they, or a complex tradition devolving from them, may have been more successful in pressing a particular idea of the spiritual life upon contemporary 'received spirituality'. For there emerges between those wallowing in the vexations of secular life and those enjoying the vision of God in which the blessed share, a distinctive intermediate position of those who are *in via*. It is here that we may be more readily persuaded by Augustine's picture, for while none in this life is likely to reach the 'homeland', serious sojourners in the spiritual life may nonetheless establish themselves on the way. A hierarchy is established which privileges the detached life over that of human affection and its attendant disruption, and it is no coincidence that this spiritual hierarchy can be mapped on to other orderings. It is not simply a contrast between the cloistered life and the secular life, but is aligned with the distinction, common to ancient philosophy, which contrasts the demands and turmoil of ordinary domestic life with the excellences of the life of the *polis*—the life according to reason, the life of the philosopher, the citizen, and the lover of immaterial beauty. Such distinctions in classical antiquity ran along overt lines of sex and class. Women, children, and slaves, as inhabitants of the rational *demi-monde*, pursue life's necessities. Adult, male, free citizens pursue what Taylor calls the 'good life: cloister, academy and law court are judged more suited to the true ends and excellences of human beings than are kitchen and nursery'.[30]

---

[29] It should be remembered that treatises like those of Gregory of Nyssa and Ambrose of Milan on virginity were written with rhetorical intent.

[30] Taylor, *Sources of the Self*, 211–12: 'men deliberate about moral excellence, they contemplate the order of things...decide how to shape and apply the laws.'

The contrast between 'ordinary life' and higher calling is not without its philosophical representatives today—a case in point is Hannah Arendt's distinction in *The Human Condition* between productive, artefact-generating *work* and repetitious, inconclusive *labour*.[31] Most of what women and slaves have done is the latter—the endless cycle of making meals which will only be eaten and washing clothes which will only be soiled. But even our advocates of love and attention seem sometimes to prefer to illustrate their thesis with relatively fixed or 'pure' objects. Iris Murdoch's preference for beauty as the best evidence for a transcendent principle of the Good is informed by her belief that ordinary human love is normally 'too profoundly possessive and also too "mechanical" to be a place of vision'.[32]

It would be rash to suggest that exaltation of the spiritual life (so fashioned) has always in Christian history meant the denigration of family life.[33] There are many examples of theologians and poets who have praised the daily round and trivial task. But for the most part such things as attending to a squalling baby are seen as honourable duties, consonant with God's purposes, rather than spiritually edifying in themselves. Most Christian women, for instance, think that what they do around

---

[31] H. Arendt, *The Human Condition* (Chicago and London: University of Chicago Press, 1998).

[32] Murdoch, *Sovereignty of Good*, 75. This comment is an interesting introduction to her novels.

[33] I have not here discussed Lutheran and Reformed traditions of domestic holiness. Indeed, the phrase 'spiritual life' is one which 'catholic Christians' (a category that includes more than Roman Catholics) are more likely to use than are Protestants. However, it is also the case that women friends of mine in the Reformed tradition tell me that, despite the positive signs, things are not much better for them in their own churches.

the home is worthy in God's service—they do not think, they have not been *taught* to think, of it as spiritual. And here monastic figures who, apparently, found God over the washing up or sweeping the floor will be called to mind; but these are not really to the point, since servile tasks were recommended because they left the mind free to contemplate. What we want is a monk who finds God while cooking a meal with one child clamouring for a drink, another who needs a bottom wiped, and a baby throwing up over his shoulder.

## III

It is not surprising that women philosophers, even when few in number, should have been prominent amongst those who have in recent years criticized that disengaged 'Man of Reason'.[34] Nor is it surprising that few are persuaded by a portrait of a spiritual hero who, going outside the feelings to which his body gives rise and the vexations of secular life, turns to meet God. Women's lives are much given to attending to particulars; to small, repetitive tasks like the washing of clothes and the wiping of noses that leave no carved stone monuments behind them. Most women in general, if not every woman in particular, have been concerned with the management of ordinary life and the realm of necessity. And most mothers—and indeed, attentive fathers—realize that there is something inchoately

[34] Sara Ruddick, *Maternal Thinking: Towards a Politics of Peace* (London: The Women's Press, 1990), attempts, on the basis of what she calls 'maternal practice', to construct an account of the practical reasoning appropriate to it. Love and attention figure large. The disengaged self, as one might imagine, fares badly as a paradigm of 'attentive parenting'.

graced about these dealings.[35] They feel that there is something unpalatable about the ancient suggestion that our affection for spouse and children is in competition with a single-minded love of God. That something is unpalatable, of course, does not make it untrue. Maybe our age is spiritually lazy? Perhaps Gregory is right in thinking that 'the life according to excellence' can be found only through the autonomy he advocates. Mothers of large families would then need to rely on the prayers of these holy individuals bringing benefit to the whole communion of saints.

There is an undoubted excellence to the monastic life, and the arguments invoked here from Gregory and Augustine are not its only or its best defences. Gregory of Nyssa and the other Cappadocians did not shun marriage so that they could avoid the demands of other people. Basil the Great's Rule for corporate monastic life was devised in part as a response to the excesses of spiritual individualism that he witnessed amongst the hermits of his day. Believing that celibacy would hasten the Lord's 'second coming', Gregory of Nyssa advocated forsaking biological family and progeny in order to serve more fully one's true brothers and sisters and sons and daughters in Christ—the poor. I am not trying to empty the cloisters, but rather to explore another account of *imitatio Dei* for those who don't take this path. It may be that ours is an unspiritual age, but it may also be that it is just a different age. Beneath the ancient wisdom of Gregory and Augustine are moral, philosophical,

---

[35] I am not making an essentialist case here. It is not that women or mothers are 'born attentive', so to speak, but rather that those engaged in attending to an infant will learn from this. I am using the word 'mothers' for the attenders throughout because, as Ruddick points out, most people who look after children and home in this way are and have been women. This is not to say that they need be women.

and even scientific assumptions that we might now want to call
into question. For instance, do we think, as Augustine did, that
it is 'egregiously silly' to doubt that the life of unchangeable
wisdom is preferable to one of change? This no longer seems
obvious to us, any more than the stillness of the fixed stars is a
useful premiss for science. What for Augustine and his audience
was a truism seems to us the residue of Neoplatonic stasis. We
understand ourselves to be creatures of change in a universe that
is changing. Cosmology, biology, and the social sciences all give
accounts of structures, creatures, and societies that change.
Scientists in general believe that our universe had a beginning
and will have an end. Light, hydrogen, carbon, hydrocarbons,
and primitive life preceded our own human species in this
world, and made our existence possible. And we might do well
to consider wisdom about human beings to be wisdom about
creatures of change.

And again, why should disengagement from the society of
the emotional and sensual world be our path to spiritual
excellence and self-overcoming. There is a self-mastery in looking after babies and young children. For, of life's experiences,
none is so 'unselving' as attending to a baby whose demands
are immediate, inconvenient, irrational, sometimes inexplicable, and wholly just. There is no 'arguing' with a baby. We need
to add the spiritual discipline of attention (*prosochē*) to self-
mastery (*enkrateia*). It is by being at the disposal of another that
we are characteristically drawn out of ourselves (*ecstasis*) and
come to understand ourselves fully as selves. Central to this
are our physical bodies, with all their affective and passible
characteristics. Common to our belief that we are by nature
changeable and changing and of necessity creatures of affections is the conviction, unproblematic for most moderns, that

we are animals—rational and spiritual animals, perhaps, but for all that, in recognizable continuity with other creatures in this universe.

## IV

Let us return to the discussion of love and attention with which we began. To be fully human and to be fully moral is to respond to that which demands our response—the other, attended to with love. Morality, religion, and mysticism are of a piece. Let us complement these Platonic themes with an Aristotelian gloss more consonant with our present self-understanding. What we need to attend to with love is not just eternal wisdom but a changing world full of creatures of change. We ourselves are such creatures—not Cartesian minds ontologically distinct from extended matter, but extended wholes.

Let us suppose that affective responses do not, or do not always, mislead, and that describing the world as it appears to members of our kind is not inferior to an imagined value-neutral observation of an ideal science, but our best handle on the true, the good, and the real. Let us suppose that our affections and even our animal responses, properly attended to, are not distractions but guides to what we are and to the love of God.

All life, even plant and protozoic life, is such as to be affected by the world it inhabits. The sunflower turns towards the sun. In his Colour Theory, Goethe reflects that 'the eye has light to thank for its being. Out of the indifferent animal frame Light has called an organ to be in its own image. And so the eye is built by Light for Light, so that the inner light may encounter the other.'[36] This is a point a modern biologist could make. Not only does seeing 'give us' the world, the world—in some real sense—gives us seeing. Because of light, organisms have developed photosensitive capacities. (Goethe puts it more beautifully.)

To recapitulate, all life, even protozoic or plant life, is such as to be affected by the world it inhabits. Attention is rewarded with reality. This is the principle of growth. But is this a stage to the moral and the spiritual? Not if one thinks that moral and devotional life is in a stark sense the product of unencumbered reason, or that our affections and desires are delusions and snares on our path to the real. Nor yet if one follows what Martha Craven Nussbaum calls Plato's 'double story' with its split between *nous* on the one hand and brute necessity on the other, and the correlative split between human beings and the other animals. Here the 'self-moving, purely active, self-suffi-cient intellect, generator of valuable acts' confronts 'bodily appetites, which are themselves passive and entirely unselect-ive, simply pushed into existence by the world and pushing, in turn, the passive agent'.[37] A familiar picture, but one in which, as it was Aristotle's genius to point out, it is difficult to explain animal motion. According to Aristotle's observations, animals, even human animals, act on the basis of desires, and the study of animal motion may tell us something important about human ethical aspirations. 'Both humans and other animals,

[36] J. W. Goethe, *Zur Farbenlehre* (1810), 'Entwurf einer Farbenlehre', in Gerhard OH and Heinrich O. Proskauer (eds.), *Goethe Farbenlehre*, (Stultgart: Verlag Freies Geistesleben, 1979), i. 56, my trans.

[37] Martha Nussbaum, *The Fragility of Goodness: Luck and Ethics in Greek Phil-osophy* (Cambridge: Cambridge University Press, 1986), 264. Nussbaum is criticiz-ing this split which, we can observe, is still found in some kinds of modern piety.

in their rational and non-rational actions, have in common that they stretch forward, so to speak, towards pieces of the world which they then attain or appropriate.'[38]

The dog leaps at the piece of meat both because it desires meat *and* because it sees the object before it as meat. The Aristotelian account with its focus on desire restores the importance of intentionality. It enables us to focus on the intentionality of animal movement, both its 'object-directedness' and 'its reponsiveness not to the world *simpliciter* but to the animals view of it'.[39] This is intended by Aristotle not to supplant the account of the deliberative, but to provide some convincing account of the way in which reasoning and moral action are in continuity with our animal nature.[40] Rather than denigrating the animal appetites, Nussbaum suggests that we acknowledge that it 'is our nature to be animal, the sort of animal that is rational. If we do not give a debased account of the animal or a puffed-up account of the rational, we will be in a position to see how well suited the one is to contribute to the flourishing of the other.'[41]

The body, no less than the soul, is the place where God acts. For Simone Weil, the body is the means by which we encounter that 'necessity' which is the ordering of the world.[42] 'The body plays a part in all apprenticeships,' she says, and especially that of suffering: 'On the plane of physical sensibility, suffering alone gives us contact with that necessity which constitutes

---

[38] Aristotle, quoted ibid. 275–6.     [39] Ibid. 270.

[40] Ibid. 286.     [41] Ibid. 287.

[42] 'Necessity' is a term of art for Simone Weil, shorthand for the whole physical system of the world: Simone Weil, *Gravity and Grace* (London: Routledge & Kegan Paul, 1963).

order in the world.'[43] This suffering may be as little as a child falling over. Those experiences are our first of the world's inexorable order.

Once we have allowed our physical natures into the picture of the spiritual life as a good, indeed a necessity, the vexations of ordinary daily life appear in a different light, but we need to be able to read them. Weil has some good analogies: when we hold a newspaper upside down, we see only strange printed shapes; but when we right it, we no longer see printed forms, but words. The passenger on the ship in a storm feels the jolts as upheavals, but the captain 'is only aware of the complex combination of the wind, the current and the swell, with the position of the boat, its shape, its sails, its rudder'.[44] He has done his apprenticeship and can read the sea.

Nothing displays more graphically the implausibility of a sharp distinction between our rational and deliberative capacities, on the one hand, and the bodily appetites and responses, on the other, than the experience of pregnancy and attending to an infant. Although it is not everyone's experience to be a mother, it is everyone's experience to have been an embryo and a baby, and it would be surprising if this did not have something to tell us about what it is to be a person. During pregnancy a series of changes take place in the mother's body which make it hospitable to the growing foetus and future child. These range from a suppression of the immune system (so that the foetus will not be rejected) to an increase in the flow of blood and preparation for lactation. None of these changes is voluntary. They are called into being

[43] Simone Weil, 'The Love of God and Affliction' in *Waiting on God* (London: Routledge & Kegan Paul, Ltd., 1951), 63–78, at 75.
[44] Ibid.

by the presence of the embryo. But consider lactation; in the days following childbirth, milk is produced involuntarily in response to the baby's cry. But the mother may be deceived, especially if she is sharing a ward with other mothers and new babies. Imagine this scene where the mother is deceived: the cry is heard, the milk gushes forth, but examination reveals that it is not her baby who has cried. The milk stops. Or the reverse: cries are heard. The source is believed to be someone else's baby. No milk. A mistake is realized. The milk flows. The important thing to notice is that, in this example, the response of lactation is *both involuntary but also rational*, dependent as it is on the mother's beliefs. And this rational component of the maternal response is not discontinuous with the other preparations her body has made. Whereas before birth the mother's body unreflectively supplies the needs of the embryo, after birth the brain joins the other organs (kidneys, guts, lungs) in attending to the new other. Or better, the whole active being of the mother, in all her instinctual and reflective capacities, is brought to bear on the needs of the baby. Just as at this early stage simple beliefs, such as the belief that it is my baby that is crying, affect simple attentive response to the newborn, so beliefs will become more complex and result in more complex actions—belief that the baby is cold, that babies should get fresh air, that toddlers should be kept from fires, that small children should be courteous to their grandparents, say their prayers, and so on. The child is introduced to a world of symbols, stories, goals, and practices. By such means, parents, even fairly mediocre parents, help babies to become 'selves'.

This process of attending to the child's needs on the basis of parental beliefs is continuous with the simple, involuntary response by which the mother produces milk when she believes her baby is crying. What we do is the result of what we believe about the child, the world, and about what it is good to have and to be. Our affections, though in Gregory's words 'low and animal', are continuous with our highest beliefs and values.

The parents—or those who attend in love—undergo changes as well. The biological reciprocity between mother and child in early infancy is continued in innumerable small acts of watchfulness, many almost as involuntary as lactation: for instance, the scanning, native to parents of toddlers, of any new surrounding for steep steps, sharp, breakable, or swallowable objects. Parents do not always think much about this, they simply do it as a few years further along in the child's life they will not. Other acts of 'attentiveness' require the disciplined and conscious exercise of humility.[45] To attend to the child properly is also to employ the proper passivity of 'letting the other be'. The love of the parent, at the best of times, holds the child up without holding them back, for they must grow, and the parents must in gradual but continuous steps 'let go' without ceasing to love unstintingly. By such means, the rational and spiritual strangely mixed with the visceral and instinctive, parents, at least once in a while, may be 'unselved', just as we may be 'unselved' by the beauty of the kestrel's flight.[46] The body, then,

---

[45] This term is used by Sarah Ruddick, whose analysis informs the sentences which follow (*Maternal Thinking*, 122).

[46] It should be noted that this 'unselving' is not the destructive abnegation of self which, as Valerie Saiving Goldstein and others have pointed out, is for many women a kind of sin rather than a sort of sanctity. A remark of Julia Kristeva's comes to mind: 'The arrival of a child is, I believe, the first and often the only opportunity a woman has to experience the Other in its radical separation from herself, that is, as an object of love (cited by Roudiez in his introduction to *Desire in Language: A Semiotic Approach to Literature* (New York: Columbia University Press, 1980), 10).

is not just or always the bastion of egocentrism. It may equally be the place of letting go.

The child is, *par excellence*, the individual 'thought of as knowable by love'.[47] Attending to the child is a work of imagination and moral effort. 'The task of attention goes on all the time and at apparently empty and everyday moments we are "looking", making those little peering efforts of the imagination which have such important cumulative results.'[48] The object of attention is not a changeless truth so much as a moving target. Children are creatures of change and chance, and an attentive gaze on the real in their case is a gaze on a changing reality.

These points are not alien to Christian theology. After all, God is portrayed in the Bible as creating a universe that endures for a time but will end. God is represented as attending to a chosen people involved, at God's behest, in seemingly ceaseless change. They are called out, established, exiled, freed. God is represented in the Prophetic writings as chivvying them along and unsettling their complacent accommodations. We seem far from Augustine's tale of the traveller who turns his back on what is material and temporary in order to seek that which is spiritual and eternal; but maybe not. Augustine elsewhere tells another story of a journey, his own journey as recounted in the *Confessions*. We know that Augustine as a young man was appalled by the crudeness of Christianity, his mother's religion; and indeed, why should a cultivated man of his place and time have found the stories of an unimportant provincial people like the Jews edifying? But this seems to have changed once he believed that God became a man and had a

---

[47] Murdoch, *Sovereignty of Good*, 40.   [48] Ibid. 43.

human history. The story of the Jews then became not otiose and irrelevant, but the locus of divine self-disclosure. The history of the Jews, and all human history is, so to speak, 'baptized'. All human history and each human history becomes the place where God meets women and men. Augustine can write his own history of divine encounter, the *Confessions*. For Augustine God's attentiveness does not derogate from God's qualities as classically conceived. This is a philosophical leit-motif of the *Confessions*. It is because God is eternal that God is present to all and every time in Augustine's life. God need not be a creature of change to be attentive to changing creatures. God need not be a particular 'thing' to attend to particulars. And, unlike the God of Aristotle whose timeless perfection entails indifference, indeed obliviousness to anything other than his own thought, the God of Augustine, the God of Scripture, attends to each changing thing—in particular. This is the work of the Spirit, this bodying forth of God in history—in our individual histories and in that of our world.[49]

We may be able to bring together the fullness of divine eternity with our own creative restlessness by an analogy: perhaps the gaze of God is like the gaze of the artist on the completed painting. Each and every pigment is discrete, and no mark is laid down carelessly; yet this green would not be present in its particular greenness were it not for this blue laid down at some time next to it. Each brush stroke has been

---

[49] '...the Spirit's godhead is precisely that of the Father and Son: the loving wisdom of self-giving. But we may say of the Spirit in particular what is true of divinity in general (*dilectio donum*) because it is through the Spirit that the life of love and gift which is God is lovingly given in the specific history of our salvation and to concrete and diverse individuals' (R. Williams, '*Sapientia* and the Trinity: Reflections on *De trinitate*', in *Collectanea Augustiniana* (Louvain: Leuven University Press, 1990), 317–32, at 327).

laid down, one by one; yet when the painting is complete, we apprehend it in a single vision. But the painting is not 'time-free'; rather, it is a condensed temporality. We gaze on it as on a complete and consummated whole bearing all the marks of its making. People might be like this under the attentive gaze of love. Perhaps creation is, too.

# 2

# *Imago Dei*

In his own image God created man,
And when from dust he fashioned Adam's face.
The likeness of his only Son was formed:
His Word incarnate, filled with truth and grace.

(Traditional hymn)

Nearly all the wisdom we possess, that is to say, true and
sound wisdom, consists of two parts: the knowledge of
God and of ourselves. But, while joined by many bonds,
which one precedes and brings forth the other is not easy
to discern.

Calvin, Institute, I. 1.1

THERE is no shortage in Christian art of vivid portrayals of the
human condition—in Byzantine apses and on the walls of
Romanesque side-chapels, in books of private devotion and
statues which front ancient cathedrals, we see men and women
redeemed and transformed. Sometimes, more darkly, we find
men and women distressed and disordered—skewered and
shovelled by devils into the pit. Ours is a protean race. It is
not just that within our species we can find a pickpocket and a
Plato, but individually each one of us can be small and great.

This is true physically, for we all begin as babies, but also spiritually, for each sinner has the capacity to become a saint.

Within Christian anthropology, a better word than 'protean' for this open-endedness is 'eschatological': human beings are eschatological and teleological. The baby has its *telos* in the woman or the man, and the sinner has his or her *telos* in the saint. By contrast to the secular, social-scientific discipline of anthropology, 'Christian' anthropology understands our human nature in terms not only of what we are, but of what we might be. We have the potential to become what we are not yet, or are not fully.

Christian anthropology, a term preferable to 'the Christian doctrine of Man', is not an item on that list of sciences which includes entomology, rodentology, and ornithology. The extension to that list which covers our species is primatology. Christian anthropology is not a branch of the natural or the social sciences, although it may make use of all of them, but a division of *sacra doctrina*, or holy teaching. Its kindred disciplines are Christology, ecclesiology, pneumatology, and soteriology—the Christian understanding of the Christ, of the Church, of the Spirit, of salvation. Each of these is predicated to some degree on revelation, but Christian anthropology needs very little to get started—sufficient to say that Christian anthropology depends upon stating that we are creatures in the strong sense—that is, we are created—and that this implies a Creator, and a Creator understood to be good.

Christian anthropology is closely related to two other branches of holy teaching. The first is 'theology', a term used generally to cover all manner of religious thought, but which here means 'the doctrine of God'. Christian anthropology is close to theology not because we are so very God-like, but because we are created by God, and our destiny—the destiny of all reasoning creatures, according to Aquinas—is to share in the life of God. Augustine makes the same point a supplication: 'Our hearts are restless until they rest in Thee.' This creaturely *telos* is as real for Augustine and Aquinas as that of the acorn to grow in to an oak, with the difference that human beings, uniquely amongst creatures, have the freedom to turn away from God, their true end.[1] Human beings are growing, changing things—destined to become what they are not, yet they are also 'God-like' in the sense that they are 'made in the image of God' (Gen. 1: 26–7). Theologians and rabbis have puzzled for centuries over this mysterious claim. In pagan antiquity the world was held to be the image of God, and man an image of the world—a microcosm. By contrast, the Bible offers the world no such glory. It is wondrous as the work of God's hands, but neither the cosmos nor anything within it is to be venerated as divine.[2] We may read of God's ways in creation, but God's image is given only to humankind.

How can this be so? Can this image be physical if God does not have a physical body? Might it be in virtue of rationality or mind, or the soul, our freedom, our possibility of self-determination, or in our capacity to make moral judgements?

---

[1] God is complete fullness of Being, abundant, outpouring life, whereas we are seeking, questing creatures. Put metaphysically, in God there are no accidents. Put positively from our point of view, we are designed to grow physiologically, morally, and spiritually.

[2] This transition is the theme of much of R. Brague, *The Wisdom of the World: The Human Experience of the Universe in Western Thought,* trans. T. L. Fagan, (Chicago and London: University of Chicago Press, 2003); see esp. ch. 11.

All of these have been suggested.[3] Mind or rationality has been the favoured candidate in Western Christianity, put in place by the mental analogies of Augustine's *De Trinitate* and subsequently reinforced (and distorted) in modernity by a Cartesian hyper-Platonism which made the mind seem 'spiritual' and the body only physical. Rabbinic sources show some hesitancy in speaking of man as in the image of God at all, fearful, it seems, of anthropomorphism.[4] It may even be that the Priestly writers whom we believe to be responsible for the Genesis texts were deliberately vague on the matter, clouding the waters in their mention of both an 'image' (*selem*) and a 'likeness' (*demut*) because, while wanting to distinguish humankind from the animals, they were reluctant to specify the precise nature of the divine 'image' in man.[5]

In Paul's writings especially the image becomes dynamic. The image is not something we wholly and simply possess, for it is Christ who is truly the image of the invisible God. The faithful are in the process of being 'conformed to the image' of the Son (Rom. 8: 29).

And all of us, with unveiled faces, seeing the glory of the Lord as though reflected in a mirror, are being transformed into the same image from one degree of glory to another; for this comes from the Lord, the Spirit (2 Cor. 3: 18).[6]

---

[3] See Karl Barth, *Church Dogmatics*, III. 1: *The Doctrine of Creation*, ed. G. W. Bromiley and T. F. Torrance (Edinburgh: T. & T. Clark, 1961), 191–205 for a broad trawl of possibilities.

[4] See Alexander Altmann, '"Homo Imago Dei" in Jewish and Christian Theology', *Journal of Religion*, 38/3 (1968), 235–59, at 235–40.

[5] See J. Barr, 'The Image of God in the Book of Genesis: A Study of Terminology', John Rylands *University of Manchester Bulletin*, 51 (Autumn 1968).

[6] Tikva Frymer-Kensky credits St Paul with introducing this 'dynamic and relative sense' of the image. Whether it is St Paul alone, it is certainly an important

Some Orthodox theologians suggest, to my mind convincingly, that to say 'man is in the image of God' is to say that 'man is mystery' because God is mystery.[7] On this reading, attractively, we do not know who or what we are—positively as well as negatively. 'Know thyself' is, after all, a pagan injunction[8] and at least post-Freud, a strict impossibility. St Paul's psychological realism in Rom. 7: 19—'For I do not do the good I want, but the evil I do not want is what I do'—is instantly familiar. Much has been made of the negative aspects of 'not knowing who we are', but in Christian teaching this has positive meaning as well, and one which is at the heart of faith: 'Beloved, we are God's children now; what we will be has not yet been revealed. What we do know is this: when he is revealed, we will be like him' (1 John 3: 2–3).

This brings us to the second of the theological subdivisions to which Christian 'anthropology' is nearly related— 'Christology'—and to sexual difference. Around the main door of Bologna's cathedral, the Basilica di S. Petronio, run a

feature of Christian thought. Frymer-Kensky says: 'When the Rabbis talk about "lessening the image", they are referring to the quantity of humans in the world, for all of us are the image. Paul on the other hand, speaks about quality, for each of us can be more of the image' (*Studies in Bible and Feminist Criticism* (Philadelphia: The Jewish Publication Society, 2006), 94). Whether introduced by Paul alone, this dynamism is a striking feature of Christian teaching on the image.

[7] Andrew Louth has used this to good effect in arguments about manipulation of embryos in reproductive technology.

[8] Contrast this maxim of ancient philosophy with Augustine in the *Confessions*. As a brash and successful young rhetorician, he *thinks* he knows himself. It is only when he embraces Christian faith that he has painfully to admit that he is, and remains, a mystery to himself. See also Thomas Cranmer's beautiful liturgical expression of the same in the *Book of Common Prayer*:

We have followed too much the devices and desires of our own hearts.
We have offended against thy holy laws.
We have left undone those things which we ought to have done;
and we have done those things which we ought not to have done.

series of carved stone tablets: on the left, the creation of Adam and of Eve, the temptation of the serpent, expulsion from the Garden; on the right, the manger, the visit of the shepherds, and that of the Magi. The whole magnificent series, executed by Jacopo della Quercia between 1425 and 1438, shows our human history: the first creation on the left of the portal, and our new creation in Christ on the right. But it is to della Quercia's representation of the creation of Eve that I wish to draw attention.

Adam is asleep on the left, turned away from the centre of the carving where God—clearly the Triune God, since he has a triangular halo—is drawing Eve out of Adam's side. It is a very statuesque 'Eve'. Although not yet risen to her full height, it is clear that when Eve does so, she will be exactly the same height as God. Indeed, she has the same distinctive aquiline nose as God, the same lips, and much the same hair. She has feminine and more youthful versions of God's eyes and God's mouth. She is fully in the image of God.

The artist has brought together two Genesis texts: Gen. 1: 26–7 ('Then God said, "Let us make humankind in our image, according to our likeness, and let them have dominion..." So God created humankind in his image, in the image of God he created them; male and female he created them') and Gen. 2: 18–23 where, having created the earth, the plants, and *Ha' adam*, the earth creature, God sees that it is not good for Ha'adam to be alone. God then creates the animals and birds and, when Ha'adam fails to find one amongst them to be his partner, at last the 'woman' from the man's side (*ishshah* from *ish* in Hebrew). The hymn which prefaces this chapter suggests that the man, Adam, is the likeness of God. Della Quercia, perhaps because he is an artist, notes that in the biblical text the image is ascribed to humankind, male and female, and not to the man alone.[9]

Della Quercia's carving captures the moment before Adam wakes to say 'this at last is bone of my bone and flesh of my flesh'. Adam sleeps soundly on while Eve and her Creator enjoy a quiet dawn of creation, *tête-à-tête*, and God delights in his newest creature.

Philosophical theologians do not characteristically treat the first books of Genesis as historical or scientific fact. Even St Augustine in his *Literal Commentary on Genesis* conjectured that by six days the Genesis text could not mean six units of twenty-four hours, not least because the first 'days' take place before the sun and the moon, whose movements describe days and nights, were created. Those who compiled Genesis did not mean to give an account of the first seconds of the universe. Of more concern to them were relationships—the relation of God to humankind captured in the Adam and Eve and the Noah stories, and then of God to Abraham and to the Israelites who descended from him. Genesis is thus consulted not as science but as a source for certain primitive Christians beliefs, 'primitive' not because they are naive, but because they are basic. Amongst these are that God created all that is, that 'all that is' is good, that the human being is created in the image of God. None of these religious and metaphysical convictions conflicts with anything science can tell us; nor could science demonstrate or falsify them. They play a regulative role in Christian thought and practice—for instance, the belief that each one is made 'in the image of God' is substantially the basis for Christian respect for each human life.

[9] St Paul seems already to have made the conflation in his Adam/Christ typology.

# Imago Dei

The Genesis text also speaks about sexual difference. It is constitutive of human beings, and it is good. It is not good for Ha'adam to be alone. Biblical critics now believe that the stories of the creation of humankind in Genesis 1 and 2 arise from two sources, Yahwist and Priestly, which fed into the final text of the book, and they do not spend much time trying to resolve the apparent contradictions. It was not so for the early Christian theologians, for whom any apparent inconsistencies had to be resolved.

One might have thought that the Fathers with their biblical conservatism would have given priority to the narrative of Genesis 1 if only because it is first; but overwhelmingly they preferred to discuss the second creation narrative where Eve is made from Adam's side. Gen. 1: 27 on its own is certainly puzzling. What can it mean that God created man (*Ha'adam*, the Hebrew male collective) in his own image, male and female? Early theologians canvassed the idea of a primal androgyne which, or who, was subsequently supplanted by the later creation of two persons of different sexes; but this reading was generally dropped in favour of concentration on the second story where *Ha'adam* (which seems in Genesis 2 to be the single male human) is made first, and Eve from his side.[10] This was the story of Genesis 2 read in a particular way—a way which fitted better the accepted order of things—man (the male) was alone at first, and God created Eve *for him* as a companion and a helper.

Unlike Genesis 1, where male and female together comprise the 'imago', Genesis 2 can therefore be read as saying that Adam

---

[10] W. A. Meeks, 'Image of the Androgyne: Some Uses of a Symbol in Earliest Christianity', *History of Religions*, 13 F (1974), 165–208.

on his own was virtually sufficient. He could do everything, so it seems, except reproduce. Eve is made as a 'helper', but 'helper' was routinely understood by the early theologians as a subordinate—leaping over the fact that elsewhere in Genesis God himself is described as 'helper' using the same Hebrew word.[11] Woman was routinely thought of as lesser, almost an afterthought. And how could it be any other way, given the position of women in late antique Hellenistic culture now reading these ancient Jewish texts as their own, Christian texts?

What kind of helper? Augustine famously surmised that for help in the fields another man would have been more useful, and for conversation another man more interesting, and this, he concluded, leaves procreation as the one thing man cannot do by himself. Man is whole and complete on his own. The woman adds nothing new to the genius of the human race, otherwise complete in itself, except affording it the capacity to reproduce.[12]

This picture of man (the male) as able to do everything except reproduce has informed theological anthropology down to the modern period. It is, in its way, a kind of egalitarianism in which everyone is 'Adam'. Women bring nothing to the table but their reproductive capacity, and 'man' (here meaning 'male') is the default position for humanity. Thus, when we speak of 'man', we include everyone, except when dealing with matters peculiar to females such as pregnancy, childbirth, and abortion. But this is not simply a matter of

---

[11] Some exegetes have pointed out that reading 'Eve' as God's afterthought goes against the general pattern of the Genesis creation narratives, in which the more perfect creatures are those made last—sea and dry land are followed by sun and moon, birds and beasts, man and—finally—woman.

[12] This is not to say that Augustine had a low view of women. On the contrary, he emerges as a proto-feminist.

language. This sexual monoculture is in one sense justifiable, for its rests on the conviction that women as well as men are fully in the image of God—a matter not uncontested in the early Church. Early exegetes puzzled as to what to do with 1 Cor. 11: 7: 'For a man ought not to have his head veiled, since he is the image and reflection of God; but woman is the reflection of man.' Did this mean that women were not fully in the image of God, a reading that would put Paul at variance with Genesis 1? Moreover, this verse had to be reconciled with Paul's teaching later in the same letter that 'The first man (*anthropos*) was from the earth, a man of dust: the second man is from heaven. As was the man of dust, so are those who are of the dust; and as is the man of heaven, so are those who are of heaven. Just as we have borne the image of the man of dust, we will also bear the image of the man of heaven' (1 Cor. 15: 47–9), and with Col. 1: 15–16: 'He is the image of the invisible God, the firstborn of all creation; for in him all things in heaven and on earth were created...all things have been created through him and for him.'[13]

The Christological texts weighed heavily with the Fathers. If Jesus Christ, unquestionably male, is the image of the invisible God, and we will all bear the image of the 'man of heaven', then it seemed reasonable to some to conclude that women will be resurrected as men.[14] Augustine to his lasting credit said 'no' to

[13] See also Rom. 8: 29–30. In 1 Corinthians Paul conflates Genesis 1 and Genesis 3, for mention of men and women made in the 'image' comes only in the former, and the man of dust only in the latter.

[14] See Kari Vogt, '"Becoming Male": One Aspect of Early Christian Anthropology', in E. S., Schüssler Fiorenza, M. Collins, *et al.* (eds.), *Women: Invisible in Theology and Church* (Edinburgh: T. & T. Clark (1985), 72–83; repr. in J. M. Soskice, and D. Lipton (eds.), *Feminism and Theology* (Oxford: Oxford University Press, 2003), 49–61.

this and rejected at the same time the more orthodox view, that the resurrected body will be 'sexless'.[15] Those who hold the woman's sex to be a defect or something necessitated only by the Fall, he believes, are quite wrong. Women will be resurrected as women in heaven, although without inciting lust. In saying this, Augustine sought to avoid the inference that woman, on her own, could not be in the image of God.

We find ourselves to this very day torn between two positions which are each compelling but seem at the same time incompatible. We must say that, Christologically speaking, women and men cannot be different, for 'all will bear the image of the man of heaven'. But we must also say that sexual difference is not, or should not be, a matter of theological indifference. Genesis 1 suggests that sexual difference has something to tell us, not just about human beings, but about God in whose image they are made, male and female. The unresolved question then is: where, why, and how does sexual difference make a difference?[16]

It is not just a matter of language. Sexual 'monoculture' is evident in the otherwise quite revolutionary Vatican II document on *The Pastoral Constitution of the Church in the Modern World* known as *Gaudium et Spes*.[17] Sexual difference, rightly or

[15] Gregory of Nyssa believed that the acquisition of genitalia was implied in the first couple's post-lapsarian 'clothing with skins', and that the resurrected body would be sexless.

[16] That it does on the ground, and in actual matters of life and death, is altogether evident from the findings of the United Nations, Aid agencies, and other NGOs over the last two decades. Poverty and its handmaiden, war, affect women, the elderly, and children disproportionately. Female morbidity figures outstrip male in all but the most affluent countries (see Amartya Sen and Martha Nussbaum (eds.), *The Quality of Life* (Oxford: Oxford University Press, 1993). The poorest of the poor are, overwhelmingly, women, and their status as 'the poor' is not separable from the burdens they bear and the disadvantages they face *as women*. These facts do not need to be rehearsed here.

[17] Promulgated in 1965.

wrongly, is largely a matter of indifference here: women are to be treated just like 'men' except where they have different problems—for instance, in questions of reproduction, or in women's freedom to work, or to marry without force, or to avoid exploitation, and so on.

One of the striking features of *Gaudium et Spes* is its Christocentric anthropology. It is a vision of the human being as everywhere related to Jesus Christ. The document was visionary in anticipating the changes taking place in the lives of women before feminism had made much of an impression in any of the Christian Churches; but reading it now with a view to sexual difference is an interesting experience.[18] Women, *per se*, are mentioned relatively rarely, but come up where the document addresses the social tension between men and women (§8), their claim for equality (§9), the sexual trafficking in women (§27), their lack of freedom in some parts of the world to choose a husband (§29), and the dignity of the conjugal pact (§47), and so on. The document says even less about men, *per se*, because when 'man' is the default position, it is hard to tell when males specifically are under discussion and when human beings in general. Throughout the document 'man' (*homo*) is meant to include everyone.[19] It drives home the points that man is made in the image of God, male and

---

[18] Especially in the new English translation of the text which studiously avoids inclusive language and uses 'man' generically throughout, except when women are being particularly discussed.

[19] So, for instance, the concluding sentence of the introduction reads: 'In the light of Christ, the image of the invisible God, the first-born of all creation, the Council means to address itself to everybody, to shed light on the mystery of man and cooperate in finding solutions to the problems of our time' (§10). It is biological males who are 'the dark continent'.

female, and that Christ is the true image.[20] The argument reaches full strength when we read that only 'God, who created man in his own image and redeemed him from sin, provides the full answer to these questions through revelation in Christ his Son made man. Whoever follows Christ, the perfect man, himself becomes more of a man' (§41).

This is compelled by the biblical teachings, already called to mind in §22 of *Gaudium et Spes*, that Christ 'became truly one of us, like us in everything except sin' and that the Christian, whether male or female, is to be 'conformed to the image of the Son who is the first-born among many brethren (Rom. 8: 29; Col. 1: 18).' At the heart of this document because, as it rightly insists, at the heart of New Testament itself, is an anthropology in which 'the mystery of man becomes clear only in the mystery of the incarnate Word. Adam, the first man (*primus homo*), was a type of the future, that is of Christ our Lord. Christ, the new Adam, in revealing the mystery of the Father and his love, makes man fully clear to himself, makes clear his high vocation' (§22).

The unanswered question is: does Christ make woman fully clear to herself? The Latin of the instruction uses the more inclusive *homo/homine*, but the patterning is upon Adam and Christ, both male. What can it mean for women to say that 'Whoever follows Christ, the perfect man, himself becomes more of a man' (§41: *Quicumque Christum sequitur, Hominem perfectum, et ipse magis homo fit*)? Do those aspects in which a woman is to become perfected or 'more of a man' include only those aspects she shares with males, like her intellect and her

---

[20] 'All men have a rational soul and are created in God's image; they share the same nature and origin; redeemed by Christ, they have the same divine vocation and destiny; so it should be more and more recognized that they are essentially equal' (§28).

life of virtue, or do they also include her mothering, her loving, her sense of her own embodiment which must be different from that of a man? Is Christ the fulfilment of female 'men', as well as male 'men', and if so, how?[21]

In contrast to *Gaudium et Spes* is the letter 'On the Collaboration of Men and Women in the Church and in the World' sent to the Catholic bishops in the summer of 2004. Whereas *Gaudium et Spes* almost elides sexual difference, this speaks of sexual difference as 'belonging ontologically to creation', an expression which is hard to construe, but which falls just short of saying that there is an 'ontological difference' between men and women. That would indeed be an odd claim, for one can see an ontological difference between a stone and a human being, but it would be difficult to see an ontological difference between a man and a woman, unless one also said that there could be an *ontological* difference between any two individuals.

A more serious problem with this emphasis on ontological difference is theological. Too strong an insistence on ontological difference would make it impossible for women to say, in the words of *Gaudium et Spes*, that Christ 'became truly one of us, like us in everything except sin'. It is for this reason that we must insist that, Christologically speaking, men and women *cannot* be different. But is sexual difference then without theological importance? Can we return to our tradition of sexual monoculture, of sexual 'indifference'? I think not, and perhaps della Quercia's creation of Eve can hint at the way forward.

---

[21] The biblical allusion seems to be to Eph. 4: 13, which reads: 'Till we all come in the unity of the faith, and of the knowledge of the Son of God, unto a perfect man, unto the measure of the stature of the fullness of Christ' (the King James Version retains 'perfect man' in translating *andra* in the Greek).

Gen. 1: 27, with its suggestion that male and female together comprise the *imago Dei*, has yet to be fully explored.[22]

It is evident that della Quercia's God, from his triangular halo, is a Triune God. God is three in one, unity in difference. Human beings in their createdness mirror this divine procession of love in being more than one, male and female. We need to affirm that all human beings are in the divine image, and that sexual difference has something to tell us about God and about ourselves. This is not that women were *made for men* any more (or any less) than that men were *made for women*. The as yet unsung glory of Gen. 1: 26–7 is that the fullness of divine life and creativity is reflected by a human race which is male and female, which encompasses if not an ontological then a primal difference.

In the midst of his *Speeches on Religion to its Cultured Despisers* Friedrich Schleiermacher provides, without explanation, this brief 'midrash' on Genesis:

Let me disclose to you a secret that lies concealed in one of the most ancient sources of poetry and religion. As long as the first man was alone with himself and nature, the deity did indeed rule over him; it addressed the man in various ways, but he did not understand it, for he did not answer it; his paradise was beautiful and the stars shone down on him from a beautiful heaven, but the sense for the world did not open within him; he did not even develop within his soul but his heart was moved by a longing for a world, and so he gathered before him the animal creation to see if one might perhaps be formed from it. Since the deity recognized that his world would be nothing so long as man was alone, it created for him a partner, and now, for the first

---

[22] The idea that human beings are made in the *image of God* is expressed only in Genesis 1, where it is said that they are made in God's image, male and female—the 'Adam's rib' narrative of Genesis 2 says nothing of the 'imago'. See Karl Barth's influential analysis of this passage in *Church Dogmatics*, III. 1.

time, the world rose before his eyes. In the flesh of his flesh and bone of his bone he discovered humanity, and in humanity the world; from this moment on he became capable of hearing the voice of the deity and of answering it, and the most sacrilegious transgression of its laws from now on no longer precluded him from association with the eternal being.[23]

Schleiermacher never identifies the 'flesh of Adam's flesh' as woman. His point is not that man needs woman (a position that Karl Barth slips into), but that to be fully human, even to praise God, we need others who are different from ourselves.[24] Were Adam alone in the garden, he would not only be unable to reproduce, he would not speak, for speech is a pre-eminently social possession. And without speech there would be no praise, no prayer—no 'world'.

We become ourselves through being with others. They conceive and give birth to us, teach us to speak and to write. Whatever meaning we give it, the startling divine plural of Gen. 1: 26, 'Let us make humankind in our image, according to our likeness' is no accident. The Church Fathers saw in it a reference to the Trinity. It may originally have signified divine speech to an angelic court, but however we construe it, some connection is being made between the sociality of the Godhead and the sociality of the human race which is more than one, male and female.[25] The point is not an androgynous God, or

[23] F. Schleiermacher, and *On Religion: Speeches to its Cultured Despisers*, ed. R. Crouter (Cambridge: Cambridge University Press, 1996), 119–20.

[24] It seems to me likely that Barth, Bonhoeffer, and Martin Buber, who all discuss that reciprocity, the 'I' and the 'Thou', implied in the narrative, may all owe their analysis to Schleiermacher, an acknowledged influence on all three.

[25] On this Tikva Frymer-Kensky, as a Jewish writer, is especially interesting: 'The use of the plural "we" indicates intentionality and cooperation in the

# Imago Dei

even a God who is both male and female—such notions would have been abhorrent to the Priestly writer. The point, rather is, difference, and from within difference creativity, reciprocity, and generation, not as of God, but as of the creature made in the image of God.[26]

God is love. We learn love through the reciprocity of our human condition, through being in relation to others who are different from ourselves—mothers, fathers, brothers, sisters, husbands, and wives. Sexual difference is a template for the fruitfulness that can come not when two are the same, but when they are different. For human creatures, as for sea and dry land, light and dark, fecundity is in the interval. And this is why sexual difference is not just instrumental to marriage or even to the family. It is good in itself.

creation of humanity, regardless of whether the "we" implies cooperation between the persons of the Trinity (as many Christians have suggested), among all the elements of the divine world (as some Jewish thinkers have said), or between God and the world (as other Jewish thinkers have offered). Whatever the precise interpretation, the plural nature of the creation of humanity applies to both the creator ("we") and the creature ("he created them male and female"). Social relationship is an indispensable part of both human nature and human purpose, and there can be no utterly single human being' (*Studies in Bible*, 101).

[26] Genesis 5 gives us a reprise of Genesis 1: 'When God created humankind he made them in the likeness of God. Male and female he created them, and he blessed them and named them "Humankind" (*H'adam*) when they were created' (Gen. 5: 1–2), and underlines the generative aspect of the *imago* by saying that Adam became the father 'of a son in his likeness, according to his image, and named him Seth (Gen. 5.3)'.

51

# 3

# Creation and Relation

The very title of the Book of Genesis means 'origins', but origins of what? Recent works on creation and theology have dealt extensively, sometimes almost exclusively, with questions about the origins of the physical universe and its life forms. The covers of the books produced bear pictures of swirling galaxies or DNA, the very large or the very small. For quite a time, especially in its *rapprochement* with the world of science, this is what theology of creation meant—talk of big bangs and 'fine tuning' of the physical variables which make life possible.

The Book of Genesis seems to have little to do with these matters. Certainly Genesis is concerned in its first chapters with the creation of the physical order; but, as it proceeds, the book is even more concerned with the creation of the people, Israel, whose adventures, after the calling of Abram in Chapter 12, occupy the remaining thirty-eight chapters. Genesis is concerned, too, with order and right relation. Its first chapters provide a schematic outline of the relation of the human being to God, the relation of man to woman, of human beings to plants and animals and to each other. Throughout Christian history these chapters of Genesis have been plundered to provide pictures of the ideal humanity, the ideal marriage, even the ideal state. The concerns of Genesis are, then, both wider and narrower, and different from those of the modern physical and biological scientist.

Some of the earliest examples of biblical commentary we possess are the Hexaemera, so called because they gave an account of the first six days of creation. One of their objects was to insist that 'all that is' was created freely by God. In posing their challenges to pagan creation narratives, they sought to do so in ways compatible with the received scientific knowledge of their own day, a feature of the Hexaemera which impressed the nineteenth-century philosopher of science Pierre Duhem. St Augustine, too, would have approved; for he thought that Christians made themselves ridiculous when they talked 'utter nonsense' about scientific matters while claiming to speak in accordance with Scripture. This makes Christian writers into laughing-stocks, he said, and does great harm; for when non-Christians hear a Christian making bizarre claims about the physical world and justifying them by appeal to Scripture, 'how are they to believe the same writings on the resurrection of the dead and the hope of eternal life and the kingdom of heaven?' According to Augustine, in a text much admired and appealed to by Galileo, 'whatever they [scientists] themselves can demonstrate by true proof about the nature of things, we can show not to be contrary to our scriptures'.[1]

This conciliatory attitude to natural science strikes us as modern on Augustine's part, for in recent decades we have entered another period of amiable relations between science and religion. In one way or another, theology has come to terms with the challenges that our great-grandparents faced

---

[1] Augustine, *The Literal Meaning of Genesis*, ed. John Hammond Taylor, SJ (New York: Newman Press, 1982), I. xix. 39.

in Darwinism—no longer do we find ourselves in the place of Ruskin, whose faith wavered with each tap of the geologists' hammer. Indeed, in recent decades some theologians have regarded science not as an enemy but as an ally, and have called attention to strategies of scientific theory construction and model building in defence of their own strategies of theory construction and model building. As modern science has become more eloquent about its own limitations and the difficulty and tentativeness of any truth-claims, theologians have been emboldened to make comparisons with their own tasks.[2] Advances in cosmology and evolutionary biology have even encouraged the more reckless among the philosophers of religion in the ever-elusive hope that one day science will prove that God exists. A number of conferences have been held on epistemology, metaphysics, theology, and astrophysics.

For those of us interested in science and religion all this is gratifying but also somewhat alarming. Why do our collections of essays always have that swirling galaxy on the cover, or a piece of electron-microscopal photography, and never a baby's foot, or a woman drawing water at a well, or—to use a biblical image of creation—a rainbow? As our essays on creation become ever more dense and theoretical, there is a danger that they become ever more remote not only from what (if anything) the biblical books say about such things, but also from what the Christian tradition ever wanted to say. Biblical scholars who somehow manage to 'gatecrash' science and religion symposia are often appalled at what passes for the Christian theology of creation. Is there not a danger that we are

---

[2] See J. M. Soskice, *Metaphor and Religious Language* (Oxford: Oxford University Press, 1985), for a more detailed account.

engaged in an elaborate parlour game which, however fascinating, is one which very few indeed will ever be able to play? Is this just a new scholasticism which, despite real merits, is as destined as its late medieval predecessor for obsolescence?

As a contributor to some of these discussions, I want to say, 'No'. These discussions are important in an overall Christian apologetic, and their obscurity to the non-professional is neither here nor there. (Few lay people understand modern astrophysics, but they would understand well enough if someone claimed that modern astrophysics had demonstrated decisively that God could not exist.) But I wish to raise the spectre of the parlour game to highlight a kind of schizophrenia in the science and religion dialogue at present. For while doubt may be cast on the immediate impact of the lofty metaphysical discussions currently taking place between scientists and theologians, there is no room to doubt the immediate impact that science and scientific practice are having on all our everyday lives. One can scarcely even begin to list the areas of moral concern on which scientific theory and practice have some bearing: computer fraud, the disposal of industrial waste, new reproductive technology, the development and cost of armaments, the allocation of medical resources, the generation and limitation of world famine, AIDS, pollution, antenatal diagnosis of genetic diseases. Wherever we turn, we see possibilities, but also dangers. Even well-intentioned efforts may have unfortunate, even disastrous, side-effects. The hardy, disease-resistant crops that we hope will transform the lives of people in poor countries may need expensive fertilizers which only the rich can buy. Thus the introduction of the crops may serve to concentrate land and wealth in the hands of those already landed and wealthy, rather than aid the subsistence farmer who was originally supposed to benefit. These moral issues do not pose a threat to Christian belief *per se*, but they do represent a challenge to which Christianity, if it is to continue in its vision, must rise.

These issues are not issues for Christians alone—they are all citizens' problems, and indeed all nations' problems, since many extend beyond the scope of a personal ethics. A woman may independently decide when pregnant not to take the alpha-feta protein tests devised to indicate neurological disorders, but she cannot decide as an individual how to dispose of nuclear waste. However, even if these are not exclusively Christian problems, nonetheless, may we not hope for some guidance from our religious beliefs as we move cautiously forward?

This is the point at which the schizophrenia in science and religion bites. After some time doing research in the philosophy of religion and philosophy of science, I was a member of a working party in medical ethics. This group, composed in the main of medical doctors, philosophers, and theologians, was discussing 'Quality of Life in Medical Decision-Making'. The contrast with my former involvement with science and religion was sharp. Whereas the science and religion debate at the 'swirling galaxies' level was fizzing with ideas and happy meetings of mind, in the area of medical ethics one felt that one was entering a conceptual wasteland, one where the theological contribution was both peripheral and impoverished. Who was to blame? Not the scientists. They were simply coming with problems, one of the biggest of which was, 'On what basis do I make judgements about or between human lives?' One doctor said, 'I can't tell you exactly when a patient has died: I can tell you when her heart stops beating, or when she stops breathing independently, or when there's no pulse or no brain activity, but to say exactly when she has died—that's no longer a medical judgement.' The scientific contribution was, one could say, morally neutral. Blame, if there is blame, must be laid at the doors of the moral theologians (amongst whom for these purposes I place myself) for the signal failure to match with theologically compelling arguments the self-confident and increasingly aggressive views of moral atheism.

In such circumstances the cry goes up for the 'Christian opinion'—that is why theologians are asked to serve on medical ethics working parties in the first place. But 'Christian opinion' does not amount to theological argument; for example, a Catholic theologian might be expected to express the 'opinion' that experimenting on embryos is wrong, but with no scope or opportunity to explain on what rational basis, in the light of their religious belief, Catholics might hold such a conviction. Rather, this is seen as just one, dogmatic view thrown in by an interest group.

If the theologian should defend the opinion, she or he would be expected to do so on what was assumed to be the neutral ground of secular moral philosophy. From there these debates always proceed in a predictable way. The same questions perennially occur and perennially fail to be resolved: When does life begin? Is the embryo a 'person'? What weight should be given to potential?, etc., with scarcely a glance at what bearing Christian doctrine might have on such matters.

In such circumstances the theologian usually colludes in playing on ground which, far from being neutral, is home ground to secular moral philosophy and a wasteland for moral theology. No wonder, then, the impoverishment almost to the point of extinction of a distinctive theological voice. All the Christian can do in such circumstances is to offer their 'opinion' in a louder voice; but since there is no real conversation, no meeting of minds, the voice is unlikely to be heard.

Even in the Christian press today the discussion of controversial moral issues often takes the form of raised voices and embattled opinions, with little reference to the theological and biblical roots which give rise to, and make sense of, these views. This shouting technique is unlikely to persuade non-Christians who do not share one's views; but, even worse, it is increasingly unlikely to convince rank-and-file believers either, especially when the milieu in which they (for the most part) move is one increasingly alienated from Christian moral assumptions.

An example which to me demonstrates the gap opening up between Christian and agnostic moral assumptions comes from Helga Kuhse and Peter Singer's book *Should the Baby Live?*, a book which deals with the problems of handicapped infants and the morality of infanticide. Kuhse and Singer go far beyond simply ignoring Christian views; they attack Christianity as the dominating, restrictive ideology which has, for so many centuries, curtailed human freedoms in the West. For more than 1,500 years, they state, Christianity has dominated Western moral thought. Those who rejected it were persecuted. 'During this long era of totalitarian enforcement, Christian moral views gained an almost unshakeable grip on our moral thinking.'[3] We must detach ourselves from them if we are to address the moral issue of severely handicapped infants. In particular, we must detach ourselves from the idea that human life has a special sanctity, a belief which may be defensible

[3] H. Kuhse, and P. Singer, *Should the Baby Live? The Problem of Handicapped Infants* (Oxford: Oxford University Press, 1985), 117.

within certain religions, but which cannot carry conviction in a pluralist state.

Let me remind you that Kuhse and Singer's argument is directed not towards abortion but towards infanticide—the killing of newborns who might otherwise live. If one includes in the definition of 'human' such indicators as self-awareness, self-control, sense of future and past, then Kuhse and Singer are content. But simply to be a member of the species *homo sapiens* is not enough to make a being 'human' in the sense necessary for life to be preserved. Many disabled babies will never be 'human' in this more rigorous sense. Why, their argument continues, should being a *homo sapiens* be so overridingly important? Is not this just species-ism, and much analogous to a racism wherein killing a black is less morally significant than killing a white? Species, like race and sex, Kuhse and Singer argue, is a morally irrelevant distinction.

They blame Christianity for the dominance in our culture of this morally irrelevant distinction, and in particular the doctrine that man (*sic*) is made in the image of God, licensed to kill other creatures but not his or her own kind. But according to Kuhse and Singer, 'an inquiring sceptic would wonder why an anencephalic infant (one born with little or no brain) more closely resembles God than, say, a pig'. Their conclusion is that 'to allow infanticide before the onset of self-awareness . . . cannot threaten anyone who is in a position to worry about it'.[4]

One should not dismiss their argument summarily. Singer's earlier book, *Animal Liberation*, was a considerable success amongst anti-species-ists, some of whom—one imagines—had

---

[4] Ibid. 124, 138.

little idea that advancing the cause of animals could have such radical implications for the claims of disabled human babies. But the striking feature of Kuhse and Singer's argument is the seriousness with which they take theology, albeit in their opinion as a negative and reactionary force. Specifically, it is the ancient idea of 'imago Dei', originating in Genesis, with which they take issue. While Christian ethics has been at pains to play on the ground of secular philosophy, tossing away its myths of origin as outmoded vehicles, here we find two secular writers throwing the ball firmly into the court of the Book of Genesis.

To respond to the accusation that the 'the traditional principle of the sanctity of human life is the outcome of some seventeen centuries of Christian domination of western thought and cannot rationally be defended'[5] brings us back to the theology of creation.

The theologies of creation which can be traced in the Old and New Testaments are not primarily interested in cosmology, and throughout Christian history, although theologians have occasionally pondered such questions as whether or not the universe had a beginning in time, these were never the central theological questions. Thomas Aquinas could suppose either possibility to be compatible with the Christian doctrine that God is Creator, although he believed, as a matter of fact, that the universe did have a beginning.

The biblical discussions of creation seem concerned not so much with where the world came from as with who it came from, not so much with what kind of creation it was in the first

---

[5] Ibid. 125.

place as with what kind of creation it was and is *now*.[6] Creation in the Old Testament is, above all, order, and it comes from God, exclusively from God. God is sovereign in creation and does not tinker with pre-existing matter like some demiurge. In Genesis, God creates the universe from nothing and effortlessly. God pushes back the waters and creates the dry land. Creation is the triumph of order over chaos, and because creation is order, it is law-abiding and, according to the Genesis story, it is initially both peaceable and just.

Later theologies posited that God, as Creator of all that is, is both mysteriously Other (for God is not a creature) and also totally intimate to everything. God is both ultimate and intimate. God is mystery, and the mystery by which all is held in being: the 'You that in accordance with its nature cannot become an it'.[7] Christians believe that in Jesus of Nazareth the Word became flesh, but not, as Karl Barth ceaselessly pointed out, that the God who is mystery becomes unmysterious in Jesus Christ. If we do not see Jesus Christ as mystery, we see not God incarnate, but a great man.

Human beings have a privileged role to play in God's creative love because, according to this story, they are made in the image of God. This is anthropocentric, but not necessarily malevolently so. One can distinguish two versions of Christian anthropocentrism, both of which have had their

---

[6] It would be misleading, of course, to say that the Old and/or New Testaments have one unified 'theology of creation'. The reader must forgive me if I speak rather loosely here. See R. Murray, 'The Bible on God's World and Our Place in It', *The Month*, 21 (1988), 798–803. and also the essays in B. W. Anderson, *Creation in the Old Testament* (Philadelphia: Fortress; London: SPCK, 1984).

[7] Martin Buber, quoted by N. Lash, *Easter in Ordinary: Reflections on Human Experience and the Knowledge of God* (London: SCM Press Ltd., 1988), 232.

advocates. In what we might call 'divine hamster cage' anthropocentrism, God is the hamster-owner, and we human
beings are the hamsters. God creates the world as a kind
of vivarium for human beings. The rest of the created order
is our lettuce leaves and clean sawdust, completely at our
disposal—quite literally, the world is our 'environment'.
(This, by the way, is a very good reason for never,
when doing theology, speaking about 'the environment' but
always speaking instead of 'creation'.) In what we might
call 'divine servant' or 'divine regent' anthropocentrism, on
the other hand, human beings are integrally part of the whole
of the created order, but they have a privileged responsibility
within it; rights are attended by responsibility. Women and
men are made 'in the image of God' not to ravage God's
creation but to attend to it, both by caring for it and by
praising it.

The idea that the human person, like the Deity, is in some
sense holy mystery is implicit in the doctrine of the *imago Dei* and
is what, for us, as for the Church Fathers, keeps the human being
from 'being finally dissected by reason'.[8] When we meet another
person, however poor, lowly, diseased, or dumb, we stand before
something which holds the divine—we stand before someone
who is mystery and must be reverenced as such, someone who,
like Buber's God, is a 'You that in accordance with its nature
cannot become an it'. Of course, we can, and do, treat other
people like 'its', as mere objects, but always to the loss of
our own humanity. We do this in pornography, in harmful

[8] Andrew Louth, 'The Mysterious Leap of Faith', in T. Sutcliffe, P. Moore, *et al.*,
*In vitro veritas—More Tracts for our Time: St Mary's Annual for 1984/5* (London,
St Mary's, Bourne Street, 1984), 89.

experiments on unwitting human victims, in indiscriminate killing in war. Ironically, we can treat our neighbours as so many 'its' precisely in our eagerness to understand how they work. We are often, as Andrew Louth has said, bewildered by mysteries that remain mysterious even when disclosed. But, he continues:

if in our encounter with others we come to control and dominate them, and are not content to allow them their freedom in which they ultimately escape our understanding and control, then we have ceased to treat them as persons. In dominating them we depersonalize them, and ourselves. As Simone Weil put it, might's 'power to transform a man into a thing is double and it cuts both ways'; it petrifies differently but equally the souls of those who suffer it, and of those who wield it.[9]

God is mystery, and woman and man in God's image are mystery. The death of God will not, as Nietzsche thought, result in the glorification of man, but rather will take from women and men any claim they may have to be reverenced as participating in the divine economy. Without God, and without the sanctity of the person made in the image of God, women and men will become not gods but mere objects to manipulate in a world of manipulable objects; thus Kuhse and Singer.

It is both salutary and confusing that the Genesis story should tell us that it is this same creature, made in the image of God, through whom sin and violence disrupt the created order. Adam and Eve disobey God; Cain slays Abel. In the story, violence spreads from the human realm to that of the animals. In the Garden of Eden the animals live peaceably with Adam and Eve and with each other. After the Flood, we are told, they

---

[9] Ibid. 91.

dread them. The point of these stories is that sin keeps us not only from right relation to other people but also from right relation to the whole created order. But the earth and all its life are not, after all, destroyed in the Flood, for the God who creates is also the God who saves—a strong theme in both Testaments. The God who saves Noah and the animals can save his people Israel, and—so Christians assert—save humanity in Christ. A God who creates can save. 'Our help is in the name of the Lord', says the Psalmist, 'who made heaven and earth' (Ps. 124: 8).

The prophet Isaiah prayed for a just king who, as God's regent over creation, would be a saviour to his people, who would bring order and banish chaos. This king would judge the poor with justice and strike down the ruthless; and then, when there was justice, there would be peace. Then, only then, says Isaiah, lapsing into visionary language, 'The wolf shall live with the lamb ... and the calf and the lion and the fatling together, and a little child shall lead them' (Isa. 11: 6–7). This is a vision of Paradise, the New Creation, the Kingdom of God. We should not let the visionary nature of language distract us from the reality of the call to right relation. The biblical picture is one in which reverence for and right relation with God entail reverence for and right relation with other people made in the image of God, and furthermore right relation with the rest of the created order.[10]

Consideration of our human nature and destiny must be consonant with good science and the understanding it can

---

[10] Robert Murray puts it this way: 'The Bible teaches us that neither sin nor salvation are affairs merely between us humans and God; sin entails alienation from our nature which relates us to God's other creatures, while salvation entails our re-integration in a vaster order and harmony which embraces the whole cosmos' ('The Bible on God's World', 799).

bring to our biology, our psychology, and our natural genesis. Yet this scientific understanding is framed, for the Christian, by the understanding that we are not just 'natural phenomena', but creatures in the literal sense—we have been created. Science agrees with Scripture in this much: we are made of dust, trillion-year-old carbon. But we are dust that has come to know itself as dust, to know that dust can do right and commit wrongs. We are dust that sees the possibility, in God's grace, of glorifying God along with the rest of the created order.

# 4

# Calling God 'Father'

FATHERS, of any sort, get only bad press these days. Fathers—as fathers—seem only to appear in the press if associated with criminal violence of a sexual, physical, or psychological sort (usually all three) towards partners, wives, or children. Or else they appear as absent. Single parent families are overwhelmingly headed by women, while 'fathers' cannot, or will not, be found. Yet, in the biblical writings, naming God 'Father' is an anticipation of great intimacy, new relation, of hope, and of love. Let me distinguish the question I wish to address from two others which do not directly concern me here. The first is the in fact misguided question of whether feminists must *always* call God 'Father'. It is misguided because there is no basis, theological or philosophical, for insisting that the feminist or anyone else should use one divine title exclusively. God has always had many names in the Jewish and Christian traditions—One, Rock, King, Judge, Vine-keeper. The second, not misguided question is: is it expedient for feminists and those sympathetic to them to call God 'Father' in writings, prayers, and liturgies where continuing to use this title may mask an imbalance in our ideas about God? This is an important question, with practical and theoretical ramifications, but it is not the one I wish to consider here. My more radical question hovers around the question of expedience but is separable from it. It is this: can a feminist be at home in a religion where 'father' is a central divine title both in foundational texts and in the subsequent history to which these have given rise? Does she not risk ingesting symbolic poison whenever Scripture is read? Is the fatherhood language central to this religion, and if central, does it bind Christianity fast to an unacceptable patriarchal religion which the feminist must reject? The question, can a feminist call God 'Father'?, thus resolves into two others which are: can the 'Father' language be eradicated from text and tradition? And can a feminist live with Christianity if it cannot be eradicated?

So just what is in a name? What hangs or does not hang on a particular notation? If we 'designate' the same subject in a different way, are we saying anything different? Wittgenstein struggled with these questions as he tried to escape from the rigid and unworkable theory of language which he put forward in his early work, the *Tractatus*. In the pages of the *Blue and Brown Books* Wittgenstein becomes more sensitive than ever he was in the earlier work to the ambiguities of natural language. He puzzles over the capacity of a notation to affect understanding and even perception. He imagines someone who wants to divide England differently from the customary divisions, who objects to convention. 'The *real* Devonshire is this,' the objector says. But he is answered: 'What you want is only a new notation and by a new notation no facts of geography are changed.' But is this really so? Does the new notation change nothing? 'It is true', Wittgenstein adds, 'that we may be irresistibly attracted or repelled by a notation.'[1]

---

[1] L. Wittgenstein, *The Blue and the Brown Books* (Oxford: Basil Blackwell, 1958), 57.

What difference does a new notation make? Why are we irresistibly drawn or repelled? Why does one metaphor or set of metaphors seem to fit the situation exactly, and another not? And what happens when a set of metaphors stops being authoritative and starts to repel? In any religion where God is conceived of as radically transcendent, it is arguable that all the language used of God will be metaphorical, or at least figurative. This means that a change in preferred metaphor or notation is always a theoretical possibility, and indeed, Christian religious language like that of any other religious tradition, is a mobile thing, responsive to the needs and perceptions of religious adherents. For the most part, however, shifts in guiding metaphors take place slowly and are largely unnoticed. Talk of the Christian as 'slave of Christ' or 'slave of God' which enjoyed some popularity in the Pauline Epistles and early Church is now scarcely used, despite its biblical warrant, by contemporary Christians, who have little understanding for or sympathy with the institution of slavery and the figures of speech it generates. The abandonment or neglect of this metaphor was not forced; it just happened. Students of the history of metaphor can see other metaphors wax and wane.

But at certain points in religious history one sees abrupt changes of imagery, a sudden revulsion from accustomed metaphors and preference for new or different ones. A dramatic instance today is the controversy surrounding the metaphor 'God as Father'. The immediate cause for complaint is the growing number of women and men who find sex-exclusive language in the liturgy and, by extension, the tradition's almost exclusively male language for God alienating. Given the universal and egalitarian nature of Christian faith, they say, we can no longer say the credal 'for us men and for our salvation' or 'Almighty and most merciful Father'. This language must go.

At first glance this problem may appear open to a simple resolution—the Churches could, like industry, government, and other institutions, simply change over to sex-inclusive language (e.g. 'for us and for our salvation') and complement the male images of God with a sprinkling of female images taken from biblical texts and tradition: for example, Jesus's description of himself as a hen gathering her chicks or Anselm's address of Christ as 'Mother'. This strategy has initial plausibility, because on one fundamental point agreement can be reached by all concerned. It is this: God is not a human being, and *a fortiori* not a male human being. God is not a male, and God is not literally 'Father'. For classical theologians, like Aquinas, 'Father' and 'King' are metaphorical divine titles because they imply limitation. Aquinas restricts what can literally be said of God to a few bare predicates—the so-called perfection terms: One, Being, Good, and so on. These terms, which to his mind do not involve limitation, can be predicated literally of God, even though we may not know what their full significance would be in the Godhead. Indeed, the insistence that God really 'is' a Father occurs within Christian heresy. Certain Arians insisted that the Bible does not speak symbolically of God, and thus that God *is* the Father and Christ *is* the Son. From this followed the heretical conclusion that the Son, Christ, must have been non-existent before begotten. The orthodox consensus is that calling God 'Father' is a metaphor, however central.

Optimistic, or perhaps naive, Reformers supposed that to admit that all language about God is figurative would lead readily to the supplementation or even replacement of the male language of God-hood by female alternatives. But this resolution has proved unacceptable to conservatives and revisionists alike. Why so?

While it may be that at the level of pure theological theory God is not male, at the level of ideology God is or has been male in the Jewish and Christian religions. At this point we find unexpected agreement between religious conservatives and radical feminists—both agree that the God of Christianity is patently male—and it is for this reason that the conservatives insist that no change to the Church's language is possible, and that some feminists leave the Churches and announce that they have become 'post-Christian' feminists.

The case for those, whether conservative or radical, who say that the Christian God is irrevocably male is a strong one. On a strictly textual basis, God in the Old Testament is overwhelmingly styled as masculine—the few feminine images of God, such as nursing mother or nesting eagle, are always subservient to guiding masculine images and often give way to bellicose conclusions. In Isa. 66: 13 God promises that 'As a mother comforts her child, so I will comfort you', but a few lines later we read that 'the LORD will come in fire, and his chariots like the whirlwind, to pay back his anger in fury' (Isa. 66: 15).

With the Christian New Testament comes the added force that Jesus's preferred title for God is 'Father'. Nowhere does Jesus invoke God in prayer except by this title. He teaches his disciples to pray 'Our Father'. Over and against feminist sensibilities is set, it seems, Dominical command. But what of those feminists who find that they do not wish to abandon either Christian faith or feminist principles, who are convinced as Christians of the full dignity of men and women, and that the Christian message must be consonant with this dignity?

Mary Daly threw down the gauntlet: 'if God is male, then male is God'.[2] 'Woman' may ever be that which is 'not God'. Female titles are reserved in the Catholic tradition for the Church, the soul, Nature, and Mary.[3] Often the female is associated with the negative of a balanced pair, a tendency inherited from Greek thought. Thus in patristic literature we find it more the norm than the exception for the female to be symbolically carnal, emotional, and creaturely, as opposed to the male which is spiritual, impassible, and divine. In allegorical interpretations of Genesis both the Jewish Alexandrian, Philo, and the Christian bishop, Ambrose (probably following Philo), have Eve represent sensuality, which leads the man, Adam (who symbolizes reason), to fall. Furthermore, the supposed 'natural' subordination of woman to man, as natural subject to natural ruler, was taken by many of the Fathers to be the paradigm of other kinds of divinely imposed subordination. Thus John Chrysostom: 'For since equality of honour does many times lead to fightings, He hath made many governments and forms of subjection; as that, for instance, of man and wife, that of son and father, that of old men and young, that of bond and free, that of ruler and ruled, that of master and disciple.'[4]

It should be clear from this brief discussion that what is objectionable is not simply that God is styled as male in the tradition, but that the 'divine male' is styled as one who is powerful, dominant, and implacable. This is disturbing not just in its subordination of women, but in giving divine justification

---

[2] M. Daly, *Beyond God the Father* (Boston: Beacon Press, 1973), 19.

[3] Rosemary Radford Ruether, 'The Feminine Nature of God: A Problem in Contemporary Religious Life', in J. B. Metz, E. Schillebeeckx, and M. Lefabure (eds.), *God as Father?* (Edinburgh: T. & T. Clark; New York: Seabury Press, 1981), 63.

[4] John Chrysostom, *Homily XXIII*.

to a hierarchical reading of the world conceived in the binaries of powerful/powerless, superior/inferior, active/passive, male/female. One is reminded of the anti-Calvinist remark of the Chevalier Ramsey, a Scottish contemporary of David Hume's, that the 'grosser pagans contented themselves with divinising lust, incest, and adultery; but the predestinatian doctors have divinised cruelty, wrath, fury, vengeance, and all the blackest vices'.[5] It is this image of God as distant and controlling that Sallie McFague finds so unsatisfactory. The primary metaphors in the tradition are hierarchical and dualistic. To speak of God as king, ruler, lord, is to portray God as so omnipotent and other from God's creatures as to make reciprocity and love between God and humankind an impossibility. Even the one metaphor that might have permitted more mutuality, 'God as father', has been compromised by its consistent association with omnipotence, as in 'almighty Father'.[6]

Here, then, is the feminist objection—much broader than the simple objection that the language of Bible and Church excludes women. The mere complementing of male images with attendant female ones is not enough. As Rosemary Reuther says, 'We cannot simply add the "mothering" to the "fathering" of god, while preserving the same hierarchical patterns of male activity and female passivity. To vindicate the "feminine" in this form is merely to make God the sanctioner of patriarchy in a new form.'[7] Similarly, tinkering with the language of the liturgy, changing 'he' to 'he and she', may be

---

[5] Quoted in David Hume, *Dialogues Concerning Natural Religion*, ed. N. Kemp-Smith (Indianapolis, Bobbs-Merrill, 1947), 10.

[6] S. McFague, *Models of God: Theology for an Ecological, Nuclear Age* (Philadelphia: Fortress Press, 1987), 18–19.

[7] Reuther, 'Feminine Nature of God', 66.

a cosmetic change which conceals a more profoundly idolatrous tendency to pray to a male God.

There is little agreement, however, as to how such problems
may be resolved. One might replace the 'father/son' symbols
with symbols from nature;[8] but this would diminish the personal element that some feminists feel to be essential. One
could speak of God as 'Mother-Daughter-Spirit', but this language finds no home amongst the texts from which Christianity takes rise, and is also open to hierarchical reading. One
could speak, as Mary Daly prefers to, of God as 'Be-ing' (Daly
refuses now to use even the word 'God'), but this abstract
language runs the risk of making God even more remote.
Moreover, it could be argued that any of these strategies, if
employed not to complement but to actually replace the Christian language of 'God as father', would result in the institution
of a new religion, that the language of 'fatherhood' is too
deeply rooted in the Christian texts and the religion itself, too
intimately tied to those texts. The best course, then, for the
feminist who cannot accept the language of 'divine fatherhood'
may be to tinker no further with models of God but to abandon Christianity, a step from which post-Christian feminists
have not shrunk. And as for feminists, myself among them,
who find that they cannot leave Christianity, must we accept all
the apparatus of patriarchal religion if we accept the language
of God's fatherhood? Is there not another way, a way by which
the language of divine fatherhood may be detached from the
male idol of a patriarchal religion? This is what I would now
like to explore.

---

[8] Dorothee Solle, 'Paternalistic Religion as Experienced by Women', in Metz
*et al.* (eds.), *God as Father?*, 73.

I am encouraged by an article of Paul Ricoeur's, 'Fatherhood: From Phantasm to Symbol'. One of his central theses is that the 'father figure is not a well-known figure whose meaning is invariable and which we can pursue in its avatars, its disappearance and return under diverse masks; it is a problematic figure, incomplete and in suspense. It is a *designation* that is susceptible of traversing a diversity of semantic levels'[9] He applies his arguments to three fields: psychoanalysis (Freud), the phenomenology of Spirit (Hegel), and the philosophy of religion. It is the treatment of this last that most concerns us here.

In discussing the 'Dialectic of Divine Fatherhood' Ricoeur takes as his discussion partner not the theologian but the exegete. He has interesting reasons for doing so. First, exegesis, as opposed to theology, remains at the level of 'religious representation' and does not carry the 'refinements' of later theory.[10] Exegesis, the study of the texts, is concerned with the progression of representation in these texts and, in this case, with the development of the figure of the 'father'. Furthermore, exegesis 'invites us not to separate the figures of God from the forms of discourse in which these figures occur'.[11] The particular genre, whether saga, myth, prophecy, hymn, or psalm, is important, because the designation of God differs according to the manner in which he is designated; whether God is described as agent, or spoken on behalf of, or invoked in prayer.

---

[9] Paul Ricoeur, 'Fatherhood: From Phantasm to Symbol', in P. Ricoeur, *The Conflict of Interpretations: Essays in Hermeneutics*, trans. D. Ihde (Evanston, Ill.: Northwestern University Press, 1974), 468.

[10] Representation in this (Hegelian) sense Ricoeur defines as 'the shaped (figurée) form of the self-manifestation of the absolute' (ibid. 481).

[11] Ibid. 482.

Turning to the Old Testament, Ricoeur draws attention to a remarkable aspect of the texts themselves—the qualitative insignificance of the divine title 'father' in the Old Testament. Ricoeur's observation may be usefully complemented by some research by Robert Hamerton-Kelly, who notes that whereas God is described as 'father' more than 170 times by Jesus in the New Testament, and is never invoked in prayer by any other title, God is designated 'father' only eleven times in the entire Old Testament, and is never invoked as such in prayer.[12] Instead, in the early narratives (or sagas) of the Book of Exodus, God is described as 'the God of *our* fathers' (my emphasis). The connection certainly exists between God and patriarchy and with Israelite family life of this time, for just as families are headed by fathers, fathers are headed by leaders of clan or tribe who are ultimately responsible to God. But still it remains, God is not 'father' but 'God of our fathers', and the difference is significant. Hamerton-Kelly argues that this Mosaic strand in the Old Testament identifies 'the God of our fathers' through the narrative and by means of historical association, 'rather than the mythological schemes of the Ancient Near East in which the gods are imagined to be the "biological" fathers of human beings... Mosaism replaces creation by a mythical procreation with creation by the mysterious Word of God... Fatherhood is strictly a symbol or metaphor for God's relationship to his people.'[13] Ricoeur, too, speaks of the remarkable 'reservation' on the part of the Hebrew people. The main name relation of God to the people in Exodus is covenant, not

---

[12] Robert Hamerton-Kelly, 'God the Father in the Bible and in the Experience of Jesus: The State of the Question', in Metz *et al.* (eds.), *God as Father?*, 98, 96.
[13] Ibid. 97.

kinship—it is, at best, the adoption of Israel and not its biological generation by God. God is *not* described as 'father', the
people of Israel are *not* true 'sons'. The prime name of God in
Exodus is that given to Moses from the burning bush, 'I Am
Who I Am', a connotation, Ricoeur says, without designation.
Indeed, it is a 'name' that casts itself in the face of all names of
God. In Exodus 'the revelation of the name is the dissolution of
all anthropomorphisms, of all figures and figurations, including that of the father. The name against the idol.'[14] The God of
Israel is defined, then, over and against father gods, gods who
beget the world, and paradoxically, it is this abolition of the
biological father God that makes non-idolatrous, metaphorical
'father language' about God possible. By means of a number of
other designations (liberator, lawgiver, the bearer of name
without image) space is created wherein God may be called
father. Movement may then take place to the designation of
God as father which takes place in the Prophets, to declaration
of the Father, and finally the invocation of God as Father
complete only with the Lord's Prayer in the New Testament.[15]

   The Prophets are of particular importance to Ricoeur, for, to
his mind, they announce the exhaustion of Israel's history, and
look to the future kingdom of God. It is here that the father
figure is declared and recognized, and it is a figure of futurity
and hope, a hope for a relationship that is to be. Ricoeur cites
the extraordinary Jer. 3: 19–20, where God speaks to his 'faithless children' thus: 'I thought you would call me, My Father,
and would not turn from following me. Instead, as a faithless
wife leaves her husband, so have you been faithless to me,
O house of Israel.'

---

[14]  Ricoeur, 'Fatherhood', 486.        [15]  Ibid. 487.

In this 'mutual contamination' of kinship metaphor, where God is both father and spouse to Israel, Ricoeur sees the 'shell of literality' broken and the symbol liberated. 'A father who is a spouse is no longer a progenitor (begetter), nor is he any more an enemy to his sons; love, solicitude, and pity carry him beyond domination and severity.'[16] The father figure is not, as Ricoeur has insisted, an 'invariable figure', but problematic, incomplete, even shocking.

Remarkable too is the fact that Jesus sometimes uses the domestic title of 'father', Abba, when invoking God. This title, Abba, is in all probability the designation used by Jesus himself. Moreover, it would seem to be a designation central to his eschatology. For, as Hamerton-Kelly says, the 'intimacy and accessibility of Almighty God is the essence of Jesus' "good news". God is not distant, aloof, not anti-human, not angry, sullen and withdrawn: God draws near, very near; God is with us.'[17] Already, then, we see the turning of the symbol, the God who is 'not Father' in Exodus, becomes father and spouse in the Prophetic literature and is revealed in the intimacy of the address of 'Abba' in books of the New Testament.[18]

According to Ricoeur, the audacity of addressing God as Abba breaks the 'reserve to which the whole Bible testifies... The audacity is possible because a new time has begun.' And he goes on: 'far, therefore, from the addressing of God as father

[16] Ibid. 489.
[17] Hamerton-Kelly, 'God the Father in the Bible', 100.
[18] The degree of intimacy implied by the title 'Abba' has recently been questioned; but even if it is not equivalent to the modern 'Daddy', the argument above holds. As Barr points out, it still belongs to the familiar and colloquial register of language. Nor need it be of crucial significance whether Jesus was the first to address God as 'Abba'. That he addressed God so at all would still be an eschatological marker. See J. Barr (1988). 'Abba Isn't "Daddy"', *JTS* 39 (1988).

being easy, along the lines of a relapse into archaism, it is rare, difficult, and audacious, because it is prophetic, directed to- wards fulfilment rather than toward origins. It does not look backward toward a great ancestor, but forward, in the direction of a new intimacy on the model of the knowledge of the son.'[19]

It is not inevitable, but not surprising, that the Hebrew scriptures, even apart from their reworkings in the Christian New Testament, press towards kinship metaphors. Anthropo- morphism is unavoidable in a religion whose God is a God of calling and address. It is people who speak, and a 'speaking God' will be spoken of personally. We find amongst the an- thropomorphizing divine titles names that indicate offices of governance, such as king, lord, judge, and names that indicate offices of service, like night-watchman, shepherd, vine-dresser. But most intimate of all are the names which indicate the offices of love—brother, father, mother, son, daughter, bride, and bridegroom—mostly kinship titles. The kinship of God and humankind is both compelled and resisted by the Hebrew scriptures—compelled for reasons of intimacy and resisted for fear of idolatry. Thus the remarkable 'Song of Moses' at the end

[19] Ricoeur, 'Fatherhood', 490–1. Left out of Ricoeur's argument is the fact that Plato on occasion used 'father' as a divine name, but in the sense of 'architect' or 'artificer', and without intimacy. Philo appears to be indebted to this Platonic stream, for instance in *The Migration of Abraham*: 'In this way the mind gradually changing its place will arrive at the Father of piety and holiness ... having opened up the road that leads from self, I hope thereby to come to discern the Universal Father, so hard to trace and unriddle, it will crown maybe the accurate self-knowledge it has gained with the knowledge of God Himself' (xxxv. 194–5). Clement of Alexandria speaks on occasion in a similar vein: 'For on account of his greatness he is ranked as the perfect, and is the father of the universe. Nor are there any parts to be predicated of him. For the one is indivisible ... therefore it is without form and name' (*Stromateis*, 5. 12. 81). But the tone of this 'fathering' talk is entirely different, and Ricoeur seems on solid ground with the New Testament itself.

of Deuteronomy not only includes one of the few instances of naming God 'Father' in the Old Testament ('Is he not your father, who created you, who made and established you?' (Deut. 32: 6)), but goes on to use a graphic image of childbirth in its accusation: 'You were unmindful of the Rock that bore you; you forgot the God who gave you birth' (Deut. 32: 18). Both paternal and maternal imagery are given in quick succession, effectively ruling out literalism, as does the equally astonishing image of God as a rock giving birth.

Ricoeur's suggestion is that within the Christian texts this movement from phantasm to symbol—from refusal of the language of physical generation to a word of designation, the 'I Am Who I Am', and then to the promise of kinship—is a process completed by the audacious address of the Son. Thus 'Father' is not a central divine title in the New Testament because its books stand in a tradition in which God is 'father'. Quite the reverse. It is the rarity of this name, and the danger of it, which makes the almost exclusive use by Jesus startling. In Ricoeur's terms, it is only with the true Son that one can have true Father, for 'father' is a dependent title, 'there is a father because there is a family, and not the reverse'.[20] It is the Son as first-born amongst the children of God who, in this sense,

---

[20] Ricoeur, 'Fatherhood', 479. This is an argument as old as Gregory of Nyssa, who employs it against Eunomius. Eunomius, according to Gregory at least, wanted to replace the scriptural titles 'Father, Son and Holy Spirit' with 'Supreme Absolute Being', a title he applied specifically to the First Person and which suggested demotion of the other two. If we do this, Gregory says, we no longer have to see relationship as constitutive of the New Testament titles, for 'without the Son the Father has neither existence nor name' (Gregory of Nyssa, *Contra Eunomius*, Book II, §4, in *Select Works*, V. 105) In discussing the explicitly Christian reading of texts, including texts of the Hebrew Bible, Ricoeur is not thereby saying that the Christian reading is the only or best reading of them. Jews read the same texts quite differently, and without the Christian teleology.

makes God 'father'. And it is in the Son's death that this distinctive fatherhood is finally established, for the death of the Son is also in some sense the death of the father who is one with the Son.[21] This death of God Ricoeur sees in Hegelian terms as the 'death of a separated transcendence'. One is left, not without God, but without the separated God. We can add to this that 'Father' and 'Son' were privileged as divine titles in patristic and medieval theology not because they were thought to be literal or adequate descriptions of the divine essence (which can never in any case be specified by us) but because they were understood to be names given by God. The important texts here are Exodus 3, where Moses at the burning bush asks God for a name, and, in the New Testament, Jesus' baptism (Luke 3: 21; Matt. 3: 17, Mark 1: 11). Just as in Exodus God gives the name 'I AM WHO I AM', so at the baptism God names Jesus 'the Son'. This 'Son' will, in turn, be the one to name God 'Father'. What 'father' and 'son' mean here cannot be read off woodenly from normal family relationships or the Arians would have their case. Rather, 'Father' and 'Son' function as loaded ciphers, their full significance disclosed only with the unfolding of the ministry of Jesus.

It remains to be seen whether this archaeology of symbols will bring any relief to the Christian feminist. Superficially, the language of fatherhood is in place more firmly than ever, for in Ricoeur's scheme it is this 'achieved language of fatherhood', reached first by rejection of divine paternity in the Mosaic narrative, then by the designation of the Prophets and the address and invocation in the New Testament which finally

---

[21] Ricoeur, 'Fatherhood', 497.

colludes in its own destruction and opens the way for a non-patriarchal religion of hope.

But what real choices does the Christian feminist have? The least problematic, as I have said, is to reject Christianity altogether. If, on the other hand, one remains a Christian, one must come to terms with those sections of its texts and tradition where the symbolism is ineradicably masculine. Undoubtedly the new language of liturgy and devotion will be more inclusive, and less masculine than that of the tradition, but in the long run one is faced with Jesus himself, God incarnate in Christian orthodoxy, whose physical masculinity cannot be gainsaid. Of course, it is open to Christians now, as always since antiquity, to deny the divinity of Christ, but this, while resolving some feminist difficulties, creates many others. Apart from the rupture with Trinitarian orthodoxy, it is not clear that one is any better off honouring Jesus as a male demi-God or supreme holy prophet. Indeed, I think this is worse. Better, again, to leave Christianity altogether.

The other possibility that we have only begun to explore is that while the paternal imagery remains in place in the historic literature at least, it may be seen as a figure not 'well known' and 'invariable' but, as Ricoeur suggests, as an incomplete figure that traverses a number of semantic levels. It is not a model there from eternity, the patriarchal father, but a mobile symbol whose sense develops through the Hebrew Bible and whose meaning in the books of the New Testament can be discerned only in the kinship of the believers and Christ, for whom God is 'Abba', father.[22]

---

[22] I should emphasize that the use of 'father' as a messianic title in the New Testament does not oblige one to give a central role to the title in contemporary religious practice, especially in situations where its use might convey the opposite

Jürgen Moltmann has argued that the name 'Father' for God has two backgrounds: one in patriarchy, the 'Universal Father' and 'dreaded Lord God' (here the term is used metaphorically), and the other where God is father of the 'first-born' Son.[23] It is the second sense which must be decisive for Christianity. 'The patriarchal ordering of the world—God the Father, Holy Father, father of the country, father of the family—is a monotheistic ordering, not a Trinitarian one.'[24] The father of Jesus, on the other hand, both *begets* and *gives birth* to his Son, and through him to the *twice-born* family of God. Moltmann says:

A father who both *begets* and *gives birth* to his son is no mere male father. He is a motherly father. He can no longer be defined as single-sexed and male, but becomes bisexual or transsexual. He is the *motherly Father* of his *only-born Son*, and at the same time the *fatherly Father* of his *only-begotten Son*. It was at this very point that the orthodox dogmatic tradition made its most daring affirmations.

---

of hope and promise. It is one messianic title amongst many, and needs to be understood in its literary and historical context; but even so understood, it may need to be used with caution. Those who do not see why the 'father' title should be problematic for women might well read the chilling indictment by Susan Brooks Thistlethwaite in her *Sex, Race, and God: Christian Feminism in Black and White* (New York: Crossroad, 1989). Writing on the basis of work with battered and sexually abused women, Thistlethwaite recognizes that the original intent of the 'father' title was not to justify violence against women, but says: 'For me, in my work with these survivors, it does not fundamentally matter. The entire history of western abuse of children, particularly of girl children by fathers, stands between us and those texts; and no amount of ahistoricism can change that fact' (p.114). Thistlethwaite also notes, however, that black Christian feminists in the USA do not have the same difficulty with 'father' language as do white feminists, and that a certain amount of toleration is needed with regard to preferred divine titles.

[23] Jürgen Moltmann, 'The Motherly Father: Is Trinitarian Patripassianism Replacing Theological Patriarchalism?', in Metz *et al.* (eds.), *God as Father?*, 51. I have some difficulties with Moltmann's ascription of literal usage to the Second Person, but this is not to the point here.

[24] Ibid. 52.

According to the Council of Toledo of 675 'we must believe that the Son was not made out of nothing, nor out of some substance or other, but from the womb of the Father (*de utero Patris*), that is that he was begotten or born (*genitus vel natus*) from the father's own being'. Whatever this declaration may be supposed to be saying about the gynaecology of the Father, these bisexual affirmations imply a radical denial of patriarchal monotheism.[25]

While feminists may be dissatisfied with Moltmann's strategy of ascribing to the 'father' the motherly attributes, this passage makes the ambiguity of the classical symbol obvious.

Jesus's address of God as 'Father' seemed to the early theologians startling and new. We are jaded now by sloppy eighteenth-century rhetoric of the 'fatherhood of God and the brotherhood of man', a noble aspiration perhaps, but not the New Testament message. In Christian teaching it is because Jesus is 'Son' that God is 'Father'. Already in the New Testament the hierarchical understanding of Father and Son is rendered unstable by Jesus who says, 'I and the Father are one'. The force of this subversion will only be felt, in due course, in the outworkings of the doctrine of the Trinity, but in the meantime, suffice it to say that, within the religious dynamics of Christianity, only the Son can show us the Father. Without the Son 'the Father' is not God, but an idol.

[25] Ibid.

# 5

# Blood and Defilement: Christology

Is there any doubt that a male saviour can save women? Surely
not. The Christian message of salvation is for all. Christians
have prayed their credal 'for us men and for our salvation' and
understood without even knowing the Latin that it was *homo*
and not *vir*. Athanasius sums up what is central to the matter:
'as the incorruptible Son of God was united to all men by *his*
*body similar to theirs*, consequently he endued all men with
incorruption by the promise concerning resurrection. And now
no longer does the corruption involved in death hold sway over
men because of the Word who dwelt among them through a
body one with theirs.[1] Jesus of Nazareth was, of course, male,
but a "body similar to theirs" can only be a human body. Even
to consider that Christ's humanity did not in some sense
embrace female humanity would be to deny him to be the
saviour of women—would be to deny that he was truly saviour
of anyone at all. We teach children to find Christ in everyone,
and praise Mother Teresa for seeing the face of Christ in the
wretchedly poor of Calcutta.

---

[1] Athanasius, *De Incarnatione*, sect. 9, ed. R. W. Thomson (Oxford: Clarendon
Press, 1971). The Greek noun here is *anthropos*. I have preserved the language of
the translator.

# Blood and Defilement

The question as to whether Christ might have been born a woman was one raised by medieval theologians. The conclusion, that it was most fitting that Christ be born a man, was never in doubt, yet the arguments are worth noting by anyone interested in the symbolics of sex. Some, like Peter Lombard, argue from *complementarity* (one sex to counterbalance the other), so that while Christ *could* have been born a woman, it was 'more appropriate that He was born of a woman and assumed a male body in order to show Christ's liberation of both sexes from sin'.[2] Albert the Great, on the other hand, argued from *symmetry* (same sex amends for same): death, while introduced by a woman, was really propagated by a man (Adam), and so should be overcome by a man.[3] Bonaventure hazards the opinion that since women are more sunk in wretchedness, Christ might have come as a woman to indicate the extent of his charity; but, over and against this (and determinative of his conclusion), he argues that since Christ is fertile and the source of regeneration, he should be male since carnal generation comes from the male. The *Summa Theologiae* however, summarizes by far the most common argument as to why Christ should be born a man: 'Because the male excels the female sex, Christ assumed a man's nature,' adding, 'So that people should not think little of the female sex, it was fitting that he should take flesh from a woman.'[4]

Also
p. 7

[2] J. Gibson, 'Could Christ have been Born a Woman?', *Journal of Feminist Studies in Religion*, 8 (1982), 69.

[3] Ibid. 71–2. Gibson says that Albert, and not Aquinas, was the first to introduce the Aristotelian argument that 'a woman is a defective man, and ... since Christ ought to represent perfection, not an imperfection of nature, He should be incarnate as a man'.

[4] Aquinas, *Summa Theologiae*, 3a. 31, 4 (London: Eyre & Spottiswoode, 1964).

By way of redress, attempts have been made in modern theology to convey the New Testament message in ways which down-play the maleness of Jesus or avoid it entirely.[5] The difficulty with bowdlerizing retellings of the story of Jesus is that we are left with such thin fare. Anything sexist, hier-archical, and violent must go; so gone is talk of fathers, kings, lords, and blood. What we have left is often a genderless Good Figure who (or which) runs the risk of losing all historical particularity, or a jagged and moralizing prophet who loves the poor and about whose life great (but usually patriarchal) legends have been spun. It is paradoxical that feminist theologies, which so often desire to stress particularity and embodiment, can result in a featureless and disembodied Christ.[6]

At first sight, the deep currents that propel New Testament Christology appear entirely masculine. The Cross, with its blood and death, has not been the focus of much feminist enthusiasm. Yet can any Christian ignore the Cross? Is this really the place where, symbolically, we must see a brutal father demanding the life of a passive son? Scriptural symbols can always surprise us.

---

[5] Elizabeth Johnson adopts a Jesus–Sophia Christology, and complements it with accounts of Spirit–Sophia and Mother–Sophia. Rosemary Ruether and Elisabeth Schüssler Fiorenza seem to favour a Christology from below, with Jesus as prophet and liberator on the side of the poor and the marginal, amongst whom the majority are women. Rita Nakashima Brock occludes the historical figure of Jesus almost entirely in focusing instead on the 'Christa community'; see R. N. Brock, *Journeys by Heart: A Christology of Erotic Power* (New York: Cross-road, 1988).

[6] This is especially true of Brock's work, which, despite its acutely physical title, supplants the physicality of Jesus entirely in its focus on the 'Christa community'.

Ancient and venerable exegetical traditions have seen the blood and water flowing from Christ's pierced side as emblematic of birth. Medieval religious art was often explicit in its representation of the Crucifixion as childbirth. We see the Church (*ecclesia*) being pulled from Christ's wounded side as Eve was pulled from Adam's. More commonly, we see the blood flowing from the side of Christ into chalices born by angels or flowing directly into the mouths of the faithful—this is, figuratively, the eucharistic blood on which believers feed, and through which feeding they become one with the Body of Christ. While the iconography is familiar, what needs to be given weight is the overtly female nature of the imagery that associates the crucified Christ with the human female body, both in giving birth and in feeding. The identification of women with the physicality of Christ was especially strong between the twelfth and fifteenth centuries, and while women were generally held to be more *physical* creatures than men (which often led to misogyny and worse), their greater physicality was also a way in which women were held to be closer to Christ, the physical presence of God.[7]

The human body, as a concept, has a history. Understandings of the relationship of body and mind, maleness and femaleness, conceptions of self and of physical substance, change. In the medieval period for instance, there was a sense in which everyone was thought to be male (since, following Aristotle, the female was a defective male), and also everyone was thought to be female, since the soul is female to God. Sexual imagery, in its broadest sense, was

[7] On this see C. W. Bynum, 'The Female Body and Religious Practice in the Later Middle Ages', in *Fragmentation and Redemption: Essays on Gender and the Human Body in Medieval Religion* (New York: Zone Books, 1991), 181–238.

# Blood and Defilement

both more pervasive and more fluid in medieval devotional writing than it has been in the modern period. A male mystic like Bernard of Clairvaux could understand himself in female images, as a bride of God and as a mother of his monks. He could, by *affect*, 'be' female while not for a moment compromising his actual masculinity, since the gendered qualities associated with the two sexes were not rigidly attached to either sex.

The stylization of Jesus as mother in the medieval period has not only to do with psychological aspects of maternal nurturing, as modern treatments tend to, but also with the physical side of what mothers do—bleed and feed. Caroline Walker Bynum writes,

As all medievalists are by now aware, the body of Christ was sometimes depicted as female in medieval devotional texts—partly, of course, because *ecclesia*, Christ's body, was a female personification, partly because the tender, nurturing aspect of God's care for souls was regularly described as motherly. Both male and female mystics called Jesus 'mother' in his eucharistic feeding of Christians with liquid exuded from his breast and in his bleeding on the Cross which gave birth to our hope of eternal life.[8]

Some of these devotions may be repugnant to the modern mind. Catherine of Siena is sometimes represented nursing at Christ's breast, sometimes as feeding at his side, blood and milk interchangeable.[9] These assumptions 'associated female and flesh

---

[8] Ibid. 76.
[9] We need to recall that medieval biologists believed breast milk to be a transmuted form of the blood which nourished the foetus in the womb—not an unreasonable conjecture since in breast feeding menstruation is suppressed. Ibid. 182.

88

with the body of God. Not only was Christ enfleshed with flesh from a woman; his own flesh did womanly things; it bled, it bled food and it gave birth to new life.'[10] But this same nexus of imagery—blood, death, birth, food, milk—can be found much earlier. John Chrysostom draws upon it in his Third Baptismal Instruction, once again in connection with John 19: 34:

But the symbols of baptism and mysteries (eucharist) come from the side of Christ. It is from His side, therefore, that Christ formed His church, just as He formed Eve from the side of Adam . . . Have you seen how Christ unites to Himself his bride? Have you seen with what food He nurtures us all? Just as a woman nurtures her offspring with her own blood and milk, so also Christ continuously nurtures with His own blood those whom He has begotten.[11]

Here the bridegroom feeds his spouse with his own blood and milk—a good example of Ricoeur's 'mutual contamination' in metaphor.

We can take this imagery of blood and birth right back to the New Testament itself, to John 19 and elsewhere in the Johannine writings. Teresa Okure, in an essay entitled 'The Significance Today of Jesus' Commission to Mary Magdalene', draws our attention to the precise nature of Mary Magdalene's commission, which is often overlooked in the stampede to claim her as 'Apostle to the Apostles'. On meeting Mary in the garden after his resurrection Jesus says, 'Go and tell my brothers and say to them, "I am ascending to my Father and your Father, to my God and your God"' (John 20: 17). This is the first time in John's gospel that the

[10] Ibid. 185.
[11] St John Chrysostom, (1963). *Baptismal Instructions*, ed. P. W. Harkins (Westminster, Md.: Newman Press, 1963), 62. It is worth noting that Karl Rahner's successful doctoral thesis, after the rejection of 'Geist in Welt', was on the image of the birth of the Church from the side of Christ in patristic thought.

disciples are told that the Father of Jesus is to be their Father, too. At the Last Supper they are named as friends and not slaves, and now, with Mary's message, they are told 'that they and Jesus now share the same parent... in God. They are in truth brothers and sisters of Jesus in God in much the same way as children related who share the same father and mother... Only now does Jesus make his Father and God in the full sense the Father and God of his disciples.'[12] This revelation of the new family takes the reader back to the Prologue, where believers are referred to not only as children of God but as being born of God. It is such a birth that Nicodemus is told he must have (John 3: 1–21) to have eternal life. This birth, Okure adds, has been 'brought about by Jesus' passion, death and resurrection', and through his pierced side on the cross.[13]

The commission to Mary Magdalene is to testify not only to the Resurrection but to a new family, a new relationship of kinship now established among the followers of Jesus. Jesus's words to Mary, 'my God and your God,' echo the words of Ruth to Naomi (Ruth 1: 16), precisely at that juncture where the demands of patrilineage are put aside in favour of a family bound by faith.

Okure's conclusions are interesting in their own right, and all the more so coming from an African New Testament scholar who emphasizes that her own African understanding of blood, kin, and birth make these Johannine associations especially resonant for her. The blood of kinship, she says, 'is the blood of the ancestors and ancestresses who are always alive... If this

[12] T. Okure, 'The Significance Today of Jesus' Commission to Mary Magdalene', *International Review of Mission*, 81 (1992), 182.
[13] Ibid. 183.

is true of human blood,' she continues, 'should it not be more so of the blood of Christ which has given birth and life to us all as children of God, and which continues to nourish us daily through the eucharist?'[14] Thus the symbolism of blood and the Cross need not by any means be restricted to punitive and penal readings. Indeed, as we have seen, other readings, notably that of blood, birth, and kin, not only are present within historical theology but may well afford us better ways into the New Testament texts whose kinship patterns are nearer to those of medieval Europe than to those of the modern West.

Birth as well as death is a type of sacrificial giving. Christ is not always and everywhere in the symbolic order a 'male' figure. There is abundant sense in seeing Christ as our mother, and his blood as the source of new life—indeed, by doing so, we recover a glorious heritage of patristic theology.[15]

But if blood is the source of life, is it not also true that in the Bible female blood is a source of impurity and defilement? Levitical purity laws affected women particularly. Rulings on the impurities caused by female blood (whether of menstruation, or childbirth, or irregular flows) were part of an 'all-pervasive blood taboo' which covered foods and sacrifice and effected separations of the sexes.[16] Although both sexes were affected by the laws concerning bodily emissions, in both Levitical law and the common Judaism of Jesus's time, women

[14] Ibid. 186.

[15] The former Anglican Bishop of London, Graham Leonard, may have had a point in saying that 'sacrificial giving is associated with femaleness'. Where his remarks are theologically suspect is in their symbolic alignment of this 'giving' with Mary/Church over and against Christ, and in his failure to see as clearly as did the medievals that the primary locus of this giving must be Christ. All good Marian theology rests on this.

[16] Leonie Archer, 'Bound by Blood: Circumcision and Menstrual Taboo', in J. M. Soskice (ed.), *After Eve* (Basingstoke: Marshal Pickering, 1990), 43.

were a greater source of contagion than men. Women were impure after childbirth, and the impurity lasted longer if the child was female. The birth of a male child resulted in forty days' childbirth impurity, that of a daughter, eighty. Whereas contact with semen resulted in impurity for one day, menstruants 'were impure for a week, and anyone who touched a menstruant, her bed or chair was impure for a day'.[17] Through many Christian centuries, and still in some quarters, menstruation and irregular bleeding were grounds for exclusion from eucharistic reception. How can one compare the blood of Christ to the blood of women?

The obvious point in the New Testament at which to explore the symbolism of female blood is the story of the healing of the woman with the haemorrhage (Mark 5: 21–43; Matt. 9: 18–34; Luke. 8: 40–56). Yet often curiously little is made of the major theme of impurity and defilement which runs through it. Contemporary preachers, and many commentaries, focus on the healing which takes place and on the woman's faith. Even when the issue of female impurity is raised, the immediate reaction of the Western Christian (and here I include the Western Christian feminist) is often unthinkingly anti-Judaic, something along the lines of 'Jesus realized that this Jewish law of purity was a nonsense'. So glib a resolution is contradicted by New Testament scholarship. Jesus did not dismiss the law. What, then, is going on in this story?

The modern Christian reader seems stuck between the Scylla of misogyny and the Charybdis of anti-Judaism. New Testament critics deploy a number of strategies. Elizabeth Schüssler

---

[17] E. P. Sanders, *Judaism: Practice and Belief, 63 BCE–66 CE* (London: SCM, 1992), 72. See also id., *Jewish Law from Jesus to the Mishnah: Five Studies* (London: SCM Press; Philadelphia: Trinity Press International, 1990), 142 ff.

Fiorenza largely skirts the issue of impurity by focusing on the woman's illness, isolation, and inferred poverty (she 'had spent all that she had'). Gerd Theissen, and many others, focus almost entirely on the woman's faith, pointing out that this story is the only miracle story, apart from that of the stilling of the storm, in which all three Synoptics talk about faith. In the woman's 'unspoken confidence... that Jesus can absorb her disease without being endangered himself', says Theissen, we see 'a faith which incorporates and transcends even the ambivalent and illegitimate'.[18] But details in the New Testament writings are seldom recorded casually, and there is good reason to think that the nature of the woman's illness is *not incidental* to the story. The gospel writers have gone out of their way, in all three Synoptics, to identify her ailment as unstoppable uterine bleeding. If this were irrelevant to the story, it would be more seemly to say simply that she had been ill for twelve years.

We must also assume that the Gospel writers want to tell us something about Jesus. The context is this: Jesus is on his way to heal Jairus's daughter when the women with the flow touches his robes. The Synoptic accounts differ in details, but in all three the woman is immediately cured. In Mark and Luke Jesus asks who has touched him, and the woman comes before him 'in fear and trembling'. Jesus says to her, 'Daughter, your faith has made you well; go in peace and be healed of your disease' (Mark 5: 34). Jesus calls the woman 'daughter' in all three accounts.

We can ask questions on more than one level. One could, for instance, ask some 'historical Jesus' questions: Was Jesus, in

---

[18] G. Theissen, *Miracle Stories of the Early Christian Tradition* (Edinburgh: T. & T. Clark, 1983), 134.

terms of contemporary Judaism, defiled by her touch? Did this affect only Temple purity, and if so, what might this suggest about attitudes to Temple purity? And so on.[19] But for the purposes of Christological reflection we can see the gospels, too, as already theological constructions, perhaps already Christological constructions, with deliberate symbolic and associative links.

Interpretations which, like Theissen's, put virtually the whole emphasis on the woman's faith are reductive. His own displays a Lutheran hermeneutical disposition to see faith as the crucial explanatory motif in the miracle stories. The suggestion that the women has an 'unspoken confidence' that Jesus can absorb her disease without endangering himself does not explain adequately why the woman came 'in fear and trembling' (Mark and Luke) when confronted. She is represented as believing that she would be healed if she touched Jesus's garment, but as uncertain of the wider consequences.

One explanation given for her fear is that, apart from behaving presumptuously, she may have defiled the teacher in touching him.[20] But this raises questions: Is it an insight into the woman's presumed psychology? Would the crowd have known of her ailment? Added to this, Charlotte Fonrobert has argued persuasively that, in the Masoretic Text, the touch of a *zavah* (a woman with an irregular or extended blood flow)

---

[19] Charlotte Fonrobert, 'The Woman with a Blood-flow (Mark 5: 24–34) Revisited: Menstrual Laws and Jewish Culture in Christian Feminist Hermeneutics', in C. A. Evans and J. A. Sanders (eds.), *Early Christian Interpretation of the Scriptures of Israel: Investigations and Proposals* (Sheffield: Sheffield Academic Press, 1997), 121–40.

[20] Schüssler Fiorenza, *In Memory of Her: A Feminist Theological Reconstruction of Christian Origins* (London: SCM Press, 1983), 124. Another interpretation put forward is that Jesus's power heals her before any defilement takes place.

does not transfer impurity to the person touched.[21] It is enough to say that she was in a position of impurity and, more than this, of infertility. Her blood is flowing to no purpose, and its flow precludes new life.

Let us expand upon this. Theissen gives little weight to the placing of the story of the woman with the haemorrhage. But in all three Synoptics the story of the woman with the flow is contained within that of Jairus's daughter, not so obviously a story of faith. But what else might this placing suggest? On the narrative level, it seems that more than one feature links the two miracles. The woman has had the flow of blood for twelve years; the daughter of Jairus is 12 years old—the age at which Jewish girls were judged nubile. The woman with the flow is impure and infertile; Jesus risks defilement by entering a house which contains a corpse and by touching the corpse/girl. The woman with the flow is made whole and (presumably) once again fertile by her healing, and is called 'daughter'; the daughter of Jairus is declared not dead, but 'sleeping', and rises to enter womanly life. Both stories have elements of defilement and 'death', and of fecundity and new life.

Apart from the exhortation to faith, another feature that all the Synoptic accounts of the miracle of the stilling of the storm share is the question the disciples ask: 'Who then is this, that even the wind and the sea obey him?' The power to control the waves is, in the Psalms, attributed to the Creator: 'Then they cried to the Lord in their trouble, and he brought them out of their distress; he made the storm be still, and the waves of the sea were hushed' (Ps. 107: 28–9). In stilling the storm Jesus seems to participate in the creative power of God, as he does in the twinned stories of the healing of the woman with the

---

[21] Fonrobert, 'Woman with a Blood-flow'.

haemorrhage and Jairus's daughter. In these he restores lost fertility, wholeness, and 'peace', as befits one fulfilling the promises of Isaiah, and his activity is emblematic of a new creation.

To recapitulate, on this Christological reading the story of the woman with the haemorrhage has nothing to do with a dismissal by Jesus of Jewish purity laws. The woman has not necessarily transgressed in touching him, nor in milling with the crowd.[22] She is, however, isolated by her impurity, and isolated in a different way by her infertility. It is possible, then, that the story does not dismiss purity laws or ignore them, but rather *turns* upon the deeper meaning of the laws surrounding blood and the flow of female blood. There 'impurity' or 'defilement' has nothing to do with sinfulness and a great deal to do with the holiness of birth and of blood and of life. The woman is in an excluded position, however, because her bleeding is irregular, and is thus a bleeding which does not yield life.

Why might the gospel writers wish to put these two female figures, the woman with the flow and Jairus's daughter, in symbolic alignment to Jesus? Early Christian legend and art identified the figure of the woman with the haemorrhage with the figure of St Veronica, the historically shadowy figure whose cloth, on wiping the brow of Christ, was imprinted with the 'true icon' (thus 'veronica'). The blood of the flow is in this telling linked with the passion of Christ.[23] As the cloth of

[22] Fonrobert is critical of M. Selvidge on this point. I take Fonrobert to have made a good case for saying that the story is not concerned with an 'abrogation of biblical traditions concerning menstruation and irregular discharges of blood' (p.135), but believe that she is on less solid ground in suggesting that it is only about Jesus power to heal a woman with a 'severe sickness'. The nature of the disorder is material to the narrative.

[23] See E. Kuryluk, *Veronica and her Cloth: History, Symbolism, and Structure of a 'True' Image* (Cambridge, Mass., and Oxford: Basil Blackwell, 1991), 7. See esp. the introduction and chs. 5 and 6.

Christ's garment stopped the flow of the woman's blood, so Veronica's cloth stops the flow of Christ's blood. As the woman's flow of blood is stopped and her fertility restored (she is made fertile with faith), so Christ's flow of blood is turned from death to 'new life'. This ancient pairing of the woman with the flow with Veronica suggests an exegesis of the Synoptic story that is not concerned with 'unclean female bodies', or with dismissal of the Law.[24] Rather, we are drawn back to the positive and life-giving power of blood—of female blood and of the blood of Christ—power which Jewish laws of purity reflect.

## CODA

The idiom of pollution lends itself to a complex algebra.

Mary Douglas, *Purity and Danger*

Blood, indicating the impure,... inherits the propensity for murder of which man must cleanse himself. But blood, as a vital element, also refers to women, fertility, and the assurance of fecundation. It thus becomes a fascinating semantic crossroads, the propitious place for abjection where death and femininity, murder and pro- creation, cessation of life and vitality all come together. 'But flesh with the life thereof, which is the blood thereof, shall ye not eat' (Genesis 9: 4).

Julia Kristeva, 'The Semiotics of Biblical Abomination'

[24] The idea that menstrual flow is in itself unclean in a repugnant (rather than ritual) sense, Fonrobert sees as a distinctly Christian development and is, as she notes, ambiguously inconsistent. If in Christ the Law has been abolished, then the Law can no longer be the reason why Christian women are enjoined not to

Everyone who believes that Jesus is the Christ has been
born of God, and everyone who loves the parent loves the
child. By this we know that we love the children of God,
when we love God and obey his commandments ... And
his commandments are not burdensome, for whatever is
born of God conquers the world ... Who is it that conquers the world but the one who believes that Jesus is the
Son of God? This is the one who came by water and
blood, Jesus Christ, not with the water only but with the
water and the blood.

1 John 5: 1–6

The symbolism of the New Testament texts is constantly dis-
ruptive. Leviticus prohibits the eating of blood, yet the central
Christian rite involves drinking blood. In Leviticus childbirth is
defiling, yet John's gospel describes God as giving birth to the
chosen. In Levitical terms a corpse radiates impurity, especially
for priests, but in Christianity the central icon of holiness, the
Great High Priest, is a dead man on a cross.[25] The symbolism
of blood is deep within the texts of Christianity, and this blood
symbolism of the Christian texts does not abandon its Jewish
ancestry—it is inexplicable without it. Blood is holy; it is the
life of the animal. This puts the Christian Eucharist in a
startling light if in it believers are nourished by the very
blood, or life, of God.

---

'approach the holy table'. Unlike the Jewish situation, this exclusion, she suggests,
is the result of Western (and Greek) contempt for the body, especially the female
body ('Woman with the Blood-flow', 137).

[25] See L. W. Countryman, *Dirt, Greed, and Sex: Sexual Ethics in the New
Testament and their Implications for Today* (Philadelphia: Fortress Press, 1988),
and also a fascinating article by T. Radcliffe, 'Christ in Hebrews: Cultic Irony', *New
Blackfriars*, 68 (1987), 494–504. *passim.*

## Blood and Defilement

The subversion of symbols—the turning, from shame to glory—which characterizes Christian texts does not mark a departure from Jewish practice but is in continuity with it. In the New Testament, as in the Hebrew scriptures, symbolic orders are constantly challenged, broken open, renewed.

# 6

# Trinity and the 'Feminine Other'

In the opening pages of *The Second Sex*, Simone de Beauvoir asks, 'Are there women, really? Most assuredly the theory of the eternal feminine still has its adherents who will whisper in your ear: "Even in Russia women still are *women*."'[1] For de Beauvoir the verbal symmetry of 'masculine' and 'feminine' is merely a matter of linguistic form. In the real world of work and love—in life in general—man is the norm, and woman is man's 'other'; thus her famous remark, 'He is the Subject, . . . she is the "Other", the "not man" defined by men.'[2]

Already in 1949 de Beauvoir is quoting and tweaking Levinas. 'Otherness', says Levinas, 'reaches its full flowering in the feminine, a term of the same rank as consciousness but of opposite meaning.'[3] 'I suppose', de Beauvoir comments, 'that Levinas does not forget that woman, too, is aware of her own consciousness . . . But it is striking that he deliberately takes a man's point of view. When he writes that "woman is mystery", he implies that she is mystery *for man*. Thus his description, which is intended to be objective, is in fact an assertion of masculine privilege'.[4]

---

[1] S. de Beauvoir, and *The Second Sex*, ed. H. M. Parshley (London: Pan Books, 1988), 13.
[2] Ibid. 16.   [3] Cited by de Beauvoir, ibid. 16.
[4] Cited by de Beauvoir, ibid 16.

# Trinity and the 'Feminine Other'

In the existentialist rubric of *The Second Sex* de Beauvoir sees the problem as this: a woman, like anyone else, is an autonomous freedom, yet she discovers herself in a world in which men force her to assume herself as the 'Other'. Woman, philosophically speaking, lacks her own subjectivity. The subject of philosophy is male, whether consciously or not, and 'woman' is constructed as man's 'other'. 'One is not born, but rather becomes a woman.'

This styling of 'woman' as man's 'other' is, for de Beauvoir, only one example (we might say the paradigmatic one) of a philosophical tradition which can only see otherness as opposition.

The existentialism of *The Second Sex* with its 'boot-strapping' approach to liberation has not worn well, particularly as a tool for the emancipation of women; but de Beauvoir's suggestion that 'woman' is largely a construct, man's 'other', has had an important place in what is known as 'second wave feminism'—feminist thought from the 1960s onwards.[5] It is not entirely a new insight. Perhaps the most droll and best-written account of woman as man's 'mirror' is given in Virginia Woolf's *A Room of One's Own*, published several decades before *The Second Sex*.

It is sometimes said, usually in criticism of feminism, that it is a product of the 1960s. If there is truth in this, it may be not because, as is often suggested, the 1960s were a period of great freedom for women (a thesis many feminists would dispute), but rather that the late 1950s and the 1960s were a period in

---

[5] Michelle Le Doeuff gives an amusing and insightful account of the 'miracle' that any kind of feminism might be based on Sartrean existentialism in her excellent book, *Hipparchia's Choice: An Essay Concerning Women, Philosophy, Etc.* (Oxford: Basil Blackwell, 1991). Briefly, 'choosing a freedom which invents its own ends' is a difficult philosophical aspiration for the Peruvian peasant woman whose husband has left her with eight children to feed. Le Doeuff speaks of Sartre's 'megalomaniacal voluntarism' (p. 127).

which many Western educated (and thus vocal) women, bombarded by advertising and the media, began to realize how many and how insistent were the ideals of womanhood held out before them—the beach-doll beauty, the stiletto heel, the whiter wash, the germ-free toilet bowl. The early 1960s were a time in which such women were told all the time what *women* were like. But by whom?

Kate Millett's *Sexual Politics*[6] gave expression to this question in literary terms. Published in 1970, the book's first chapter included long, raunchy excerpts from Henry Miller's *Sexus*,[7] a book published in France in the Forties but censored in the United States until its publication in the mid-Sixties. Kate Millet asks her readers to note, in Miller's extensive and excruciating account of sexual conquests (by the man) and degradation (of the woman), that the events narrated are physically impossible—for instance, with regard to the ease with which certain female garments could be shed and so on. Miller's narrative is a particularly vicious fantasy of male potency and female degradation. Following the lifting of censorship and the publication of the book in English, women reading Henry Miller's book (especially if they had also read Kate Millet's) might well ask: Is this what Miller thinks about *some* women? Is this what Miller thinks about *all* women? Is this what many men think about many women—or wish to think about them? And who are, or rather, what is 'woman' anyway—amidst the flood of media representations—visual, verbal, commercial, even those of children's cartoons (remember Wilma in *The Flintstones*)? Are there any women in Henry Miller's novels?

---

[6] K. Millett, *Sexual Politics* (London: Virago, 1970).
[7] H. Miller, *Sexus.* London (Calder & Boyars, 1969).

There are female characters, but he has composed them. In Milton's *Paradise Lost* Eve confesses to Adam delight in her pre-ordained subjugation:

> My author and disposer, what thou bidds't
> Unargued I obey; so God ordains;
> God is thy law, thou mind: to know no more
> Is woman's happiest knowledge, and her praise.

(Paradise Lost, book IV)

This sounds like wishful thinking, giving Milton's own troubled matrimonial circumstances. But who, in the end, speaks for women? Largely, and especially in the texts of theology, it has been men. And what versions of 'woman' is it that we get from largely male sources?

Around the same time as Kate Millet wrote, similar questions were beginning to be asked of the texts of theology. In 1960 Valerie Saiving Goldstein published an article entitled 'The Human Situation—A Feminine View'. In it she made the un-controversial observation that the soteriology of a theologian much depends on his 'doctrine of man'—that is, his anthropology. Descriptions of the nature of salvation are dependent on what one thinks people are like and what they are being saved 'from'. Focusing on the writings of Reinhold Niebuhr and Anders Nygren, she argued that their anthropologies, far from being neutral, were much more appropriate to men than to women. Sin was identified in terms of 'the' human temptations to pride, self-assertion, and self-centredness—salvation correla-tively in terms of humility and self-abnegation. But these, Gold-stein argued, might not necessarily be the temptations of women. The sins of women, she suggested, might better be suggested by terms like triviality and diffuseness, dependence on others for one's own self-definition, and so on—what she called an 'underdevelopment or negation of the self'.[8]

We need not take Saiving Goldstein's article as proposing an essentialism in which men are universally selfish and arrogant, and women submissive. Nor was she saying that women sin less than men. Rather, what her article did point out, and graphically for many of its readers, was that the texts of modern theology have spoken with inappropriate ease of '*the* human condition' and invoked without sufficient caution a 'universal' subject who was in fact a 'local' hero.

We might summarize Saiving Goldstein's insight, and Kate Millet's, as the recognition that texts are 'sexed'. 'Man', the subject of so many modern and early modern texts of economics, politics, and theology, is not in fact neutral, but already placed by race, class, and gender. And, most importantly, this is so *not only* when the texts in question say depressing things about women, but even when the texts are, like those of Niebuhr and Nygren, ostensibly neutral—in theory speaking for 'everyman'.

Here we might note shared concerns of some feminist theology and some French philosophy.[9] The point of congruence lies in the shared questions, 'Who is the subject?' and 'How can the Other speak?'

'Woman' and 'the feminine' are considerable topics in French philosophy, and not simply or even mostly topics for women. Foucault, Levinas, Lyotard, Deleuze, and Barthes all discuss 'woman'. We need to add in haste that 'woman' here does not necessarily have reference to actual women, but rather

---

[8] S. Goldstein, 'The Human Situation—A Feminine View', *Journal of Religion*, 40 (1960), 100–12.

[9] Although, with a few exceptions, practitioners in these two areas show little interest in, or awareness of, the existence of each other.

functions as a philosophical cipher, representing what has been called 'a new rhetorical space', sometimes also called a void, excess, the unsaid, unknowable lack, the uncontained—all that is 'woman'.[10]

The nature of this 'space' seems to vary from theorist to theorist, as do reasons why it should be called 'woman'. For some, most notably Lacan and those affected by him, it is the impact on French thought of psychoanalysis. Others, like Derrida, undertake critiques of Western philosophy as a system in which the One dominates and triumphs over the other. This philosophical tendency to reduce everything to 'the same' is seen by some theorists, women and men, as having a masculine logic (and again this does not mean that it is exclusively males who engage in it). Irigaray, for instance, speaks of philosophy's *position of mastery*, and says that 'this domination of the philosophic logos stems in large part from its power to *reduce all others to the economy of the Same*'.[11] Attention to 'woman' is thus a strategy by means of which one can criticize 'the indifference of the existing order'.

The philosophical feminine is invoked at the last stages in the death of Man—here the Cartesian subject. Described in pastiche by Irigaray, what ails the 'Cartesian cogito' is that it 'is conceived as auto-effective, auto-affecting and solipsistic'. By doubting everything, this 'singular subject' is 'charged with giving birth to the universe all over again, after he has brought himself back into the world in a way that avoids the precariousness of

[10] See A. A. Jardine, *Gynesis: Configurations of Woman and Modernity* (Ithaca, NY, and London: Cornell University Press, 1985), 25.

[11] L. Irigaray, *This Sex which is not One* (Ithaca, NY: Cornell University Press, 1985), 74.

105

existence as it is usually understood'.[12] By generating himself in an act of rationality, this cogito detaches himself and is transcendental in the sense of transcending his own material base, even his own body, which becomes one more 'object' of study.[13] And because it is, figuratively, '*Man*' who is dead, and indeed the 'Cartesian man' who constitutes himself by the denial of the '*mater*-ial' (that is, the 'feminine')—that other is named 'woman'.

It should be clear that 'French theories of the feminine' cannot be equated or confused with 'French feminist theory', although the latter is informed by the former.[14] And it is not surprising that feminists have been cautious in welcoming this new-found invocation of 'the feminine' and the so-called becoming woman of French philosophy. It is unsurprising that some women philosophers have responded by casting off the whole neo-Nietzschean, neo-Freudian blather, with all its unfortunate residual dualisms of male and female.[15] However, some of the most interesting theoreticians of French feminism, notably Luce Irigaray and Julia Kristeva, have not, and for reasons which should interest the theologian, and to which I shall return.

Contemporary English-language philosophy and French philosophy share an interest in language and linguistics, although they develop it in different ways. In particular,

[12] L. Irigaray, *Speculum of the Other Woman* (Ithaca, NY: Cornell University Press, 1985), 181–2.

[13] Rosi Braidotti, *Patterns of Dissonance: A Study of Women in Contemporary Philosophy* (Cambridge: Polity, 1991), 254. See also Taylor, *Sources of the Self*, *passim*.

[14] Braidotti, *Patterns of Dissonance*, 11.

[15] This is true of some Anglo-American critics, but also to some extent of the French philosopher Michelle Le Doeuff, for instance.

modern French philosophy has been influenced in ways in which the English empiricist tradition has not, by both psychoanalysis and cultural anthropology, and accordingly importance is given to questions of image, symbol, and the powers of figuration.[16] More specifically within feminist critical theory, the contrast has sometimes been drawn between the concern of English and American feminists with the 'oppression of women' and the concern of French theorists with the 'repression of the feminine'. This is recognized, increasingly, as not an 'either–or'.[17] Women's problems, Irigaray's work suggests, are *both* real *and* symbolic.[18] We need better employment legislation, work-place crèches, and so on; but we also need to change at a profound level the manner in which we think about self and other, about 'man' and 'woman'. French feminists may be wary of the 'becoming woman' of philosophy while finding some truth in the diagnosis of Western modernity as unable positively to think of 'difference', or otherness except as 'the other of the same'. On the practical level, any serious attempts to think seriously about difference could not but affect the lives of actual women.

The importance accorded to questions of symbolism means that French feminist theorists are less likely than their Anglo-American counterparts to suppose that one can effect lasting change or achieve 'equality' while ignoring the sexed nature of texts which, historically, have informed Western intellectual culture and whose values have been exported round the

[16] Jean-Joseph Goux makes this point in his 'The Phallus: Masculine Identity and the "Exchange of Women"', *differences*, 41 (1992), 42–75.

[17] See Elizabeth Gross, 'Philosophy, Subjectivity and the Body: Kristeva and Irigaray', in C. Pateman, and E. Gross, *Feminist Challenges: Social and Political Theory* (London: Allen & Unwin, 1986), 133.

[18] Braidotti, *Patterns of Dissonance*, 252.

world. (This, too, should make them important reading for feminist *theologians* who have even more reason than secular feminists to be aware of the enduring influence of symbols on present-day life.) Irigaray, for example, is suspicious of the rush to androgyny that she detects in some feminist thought. The so-called androgynous ideal will still be male-formed. What other ideal have we, whether we be male or female in this society, in which to think? And when enunciating feminist aspirations to equality, we must also ask, as Irigaray does, 'equal to whom?' If the answer remains 'to men', then the male is still supplying the norm around which the female or the neuter is constructed, with the further disadvantage that this andromorphism is concealed.[19] What we need, according to Irigaray, is to rethink sexual difference.

The thesis that the texts of philosophy are 'sexed', while perhaps initially curious, becomes far more convincing on re-examination of some of the texts of ancient philosophy. Let me illustrate this by reference to an article by Jean-Joseph Goux, 'The Phallus: Masculine Identity and the "Exchange of Women"'.[20] While the 'phallus' is a common notion in modern ethnography and psychoanalysis, Goux reminds us of its place in ancient philosophy. Citing Herodotus and Plutarch, he reminds us of the place of the phallus in ancient myth and cult and its close (and obvious) association with a masculine principle of generation. As such, the phallus has a close association with intelligence, or formative word (*logos*). The sexual imagery of Plato's allegory of the cave, with its movement from the

[19] L. Irigaray, *Je, tu, nous: Toward a Culture of Difference* (New York and London: Routledge, 1993), 12.
[20] See n. 16 above.

womb-like *mater*-ial, through representation to the Forms, was evident to philosophers long before Freud.[21] Plutarch writes: 'Plato is wont to give the conceptual the name of *idea, example*, or *father*, and to the material the name of *mother* or *nurse*, or *place of generation*, and to that which results from both the name offspring or generation.'[22] Intelligence or reason is that which transcends matter and the material (*mater*). Thus, says Goux, the 'inaugural opposition of metaphysics', a major metaphysical opposition between 'a male principle which is intelligible reason (ideas, model, father) and a female principle which is matter', is quite overt in Plato and Aristotle (p.46). The female (nurturing, womb-like matter) is that which the male, rational principle transcends. The Neoplatonists revived these generative metaphors in their idea of the One as first principle, fertile power, and source of all life. In the Stoics 'the masculine sexual signification of the organizing principle stands out even more sharply... in the unambiguous notion of *logos spermatikos*... the power of sperm fashioning each thing in accordance with its species' (p.48). *Logos* is no more gender-neutral a term than is 'father' in these texts, linked as it is to metaphors of male generation.

Goux's target is metaphysical dualism, and that tradition of metaphysics which emphasizes presence versus absence, the One and the Other of the same; but theologians with some knowledge of the use of the term *logos spermatikos* in early Christian texts should also sit up sharply. It is almost impossible not to see here, for instance, another reason why for those whose biological beliefs and symbols were of such an order, the notion of the ordination of women would be out of the question, quite

---

[21] Irigaray explores Plato's allegory at some length in *Speculum of the Other Woman*.

[22] Plutarch, *Moralia*, cited by Goux, 'Phallus', 46.

literally 'inconceivable'. For it is not only Jesus of Nazareth who is humanly male, but God as source of generation, and Logos, as seed of generation, who are symbolically male. In a scheme where in only males are truly generative, then, in a sense, only males can truly give birth. The only true parent is the father, source of seed which it is the female task to nurture.[23]

Perhaps I have said enough to suggest why investigations into sexual and procreative metaphors in the texts of philosophy should interest not only French philosophers and critics of the Western tradition of metaphysics,[24] but also theologians and students of Trinitarian theology. Let me turn now directly to discussion of the doctrine of the Trinity.

The doctrine of the Trinity has always been contested. Its formulation was late, its overt biblical basis slight, and its reliance on metaphysics substantial. In the last 300 years of Western Christianity, a number of theologians have thought that the doctrine has outworn its usefulness and should be scrapped. A frequent criticism from the feminist quarter is that the doctrine of the Trinity is used to reinforce hierarchy and underwrite the maleness of God. Paradoxically, the original motives for the doctrine were to subvert hierarchical

[23] Aquinas, in the *Contra Gentiles*, suggests that one reason why we do not speak of the First Person of the Trinity as *Mother* is because God begets actively, and the role of the mother in procreation is passive (IV. 11.19, p. 90).

[24] Nicholas Lash has rightly, insistently, and one might even say doggedly pointed out how unsatisfactory it is for philosophers to speak so generally of '*the* Western tradition of metaphysics' or '*the* onto-theological constitution of metaphysics', as though the same story could be told across 2,500 years. It is, more accurately, one particular, and we could say in the modern period particularly dominant, tradition of Western metaphysics that is being criticized. Those who speak of '*the* Western tradition' often seem forgetful, in a way one hopes theologians are not, of medieval philosophy. Indeed, part of the argument here is that recollection of the delicate philosophical arguments on the Trinity itself might be a sovereign cure against any system which degenerates into *oppositional dualisms*.

readings, not reinforce them, especially when these involved the subordination of the Second Person. An all-powerful male eminence is not the favoured picture of God for feminists, nor for Trinitarian orthodoxy.

Yet it is not difficult to see why some modern theologians, and not just feminist ones, have felt that the doctrine underwrites hierarchy. Trinitarian formulae can often, apart from the specific historical contexts from which they arose, suggest their opposites. Talk of 'triunity' readily appears to be tritheism. Walter Kasper writes with great caution and accuracy of the absolute unity of God *despite* the distinction of Persons, and the absolute quality of the Persons *despite* the dependence of the Second Person on the First and the Third on the First and the Second, and so on. To many people this 'despite' language sounds a little like Orwell's *Animal Farm*: all animals are equal, but some are more equal than others. Trinitarian language may be introduced, historically, as a corrective to the tendency to idolatry, but how successful has it been? Tritheism may have been despatched early on, but more subtle forms of subordinationism, monarchianism, and deism, all in their way idolatrous, have enjoyed good careers. Feminist criticisms of classical formulations of the doctrine vary from simple rejection of what sounds like a three-men club, to more nuanced critiques of the way in which, despite best efforts, the Father always seems to be accorded a status superior to the other two Persons, with the Holy Spirit as a distinct third. The Trinity appears still hierarchical, still male—maleness, indeed, seems enshrined in God's eternity.[25]

---

[25] For this kind of criticism see M. Grey, 'The Core of our Desire: Re-Imaging the Trinity', *Theology*, 93 (1990), 363–72.

## Trinity and the 'Feminine Other'

How can we name the Triune God when the Trinitarian confession seems to take the language of fatherhood and sonship right into the eternal life of God? One strategy has been to feminize the Spirit. We can readily uncover a tradition of regarding the Spirit as the maternal aspect of God—brooding, nurturing, bringing new members of the Church to life in baptism. There is also the early Syriac tradition of styling the Spirit as feminine, following the female gender of the noun in the Semitic languages (*ruha'* in Syriac, *ruâh* in Hebrew). These attempts have generally failed to convince feminist and other theologians of their enduring merit for women or, for that matter, for the Trinity. Consider the implications of these remarks of Yves Congar:

The part played in our upbringing by the Holy Spirit is that of a mother—a mother who enables us to know our Father, God, and our brother, Jesus . . . He (the Spirit) teaches us how to practise the virtues and how to use the gifts of a son of God by grace. All this is part of a mother's function.[26]

Along with deifying one particular, modern Western version of 'a mother's function' (why is it not a mother's function to raise the crops so that her family may eat?), the Spirit by implication is helpmeet to the other two Persons, who are really there to be known and loved.[27] Feminists are surely right to reject what Sarah Coakley has called 'mawkish and sentimentalised

---

[26] Y. Congar, *I Believe in the Holy Spirit* (London: Chapman, 1983), 161.

[27] Even less satisfactory, as Elizabeth Johnson notes, is the valiant effort by the process theologian John Cobb to align the Logos, as the masculine aspect of God, with order, novelty, demand, agency, and transformation, while the feminine aspect of God, the kingdom or Spirit, is linked with receptivity, empathy, suffering, and preservation. See E. A. Johnson, 'The Incomprehensibility of God and the Image of God Male and Female', *Theological Studies*, 45 (1984), 459.

versions of the feminine' as both providing warrant for a particular stereotype of the feminine and at the same time feeding the unorthodox suggestion that there is sexual difference in the Trinity. Furthermore, this kind of feminizing rhetoric does nothing to counteract the genuine neglect of the Spirit in modern theology, in which the Spirit appears as a sort of 'edifying appendage' to the two real Persons, those who have faces, the Father and the Son.[28] We must avoid, as Coakley says, subordinating 'the Spirit to a Father who, as "cause", and "source" of the other two persons, remains as a "masculine" stereotype with the theological upper hand'.[29] Fear of covert monarchianism is a sound theological instinct.

It is important, however, to see that the 'Father' and 'Son' language is not kept in place by the doctrine of the Trinity, but the other way round. The doctrine of the Trinity is precisely the reflective means by which unacceptable inferences from the primary language of the New Testament have been kept in place: for instance, the unacceptable inference from the fact that there are three names—Father, Son, and Spirit—to the conclusion that there are three Gods, or the unacceptable inference from a Father who is ungenerate and a Son begotten to the idea that the Father must be superior to the Son. It was of the essence to the earliest defences of the doctrine that the Godhead be understood as life, love, and complete mutuality— the Son is not less than the Father, nor can the Father be Father without Son and Spirit. The Trinity qualifies all our presumptive knowledge of God. For Gregory of Nyssa even the threefold

---

[28] Ibid. 457.
[29] S. Coakley, ' "Femininity" and the Holy Spirit?', in M. Furlong (ed.), *Mirror to the Church: Reflections on Sexism* (London: SPCK, 1988), 124–35.

naming, Father, Son, and Holy Spirit, does not describe the divine essence, something that could never be done.

Well-meant attempts at inclusiveness which feminize the Spirit almost always introduce unacceptable difference between the three Persons. The more orthodox strategy is to style all three Persons of the Trinity as feminine as well as masculine. Susan Ashbrook Harvey points out that Syriac Christians, in feminizing the Spirit, did not posit a female deity alongside or in distinction to a male deity. Such concrete identities were available in the pagan deities of the Syrian Orient, 'where a triad of mother, father, and son was a common configuration of divinity'.[30] While the Spirit was styled as feminine, and occasionally identified with the Wisdom figure, the feminization was drawn across all three Persons of the Trinity. The *Odes of Solomon*, probably from the second Christian century have a maternal Spirit but also a maternal Father:

> A cup of milk was offered to me
> And I drank it with the sweetness of the Lord's kindness.
> The Son is the cup,
> And He who was milked is the Father,
> And she who milked Him is the Holy Spirit,

Harvey highlights the wealth of bodily and gendered metaphors, but also the way in which they are layered in paradoxical and conflicting sequences: 'Roles are reversed, fused, inverted: no one is simply who they seem to be. More accurately, everyone is *more than* they seem to be—Mary is more than a woman in what she does; the Father and the Spirit are more than one

[30] S. Ashbrook Harvey (1993). 'Feminine Imagery for the Divine: The Holy Spirit, the Odes of Solomon, and early Syriac Tradition', *St Vladimir's Theological Quarterly*, 37/2–3 (1993), 114.

gender can convey in the effort to glimpse their works. Gender is thus shown to be important, even crucial, to identity—but not one specific gender.'[31] In this rhetorical excess, God is not lacking gender but exceeds gender—that to which our human experience of gender and physicality feebly but really points. The further theological incentive, for we cannot imagine that early Syriac theologians were much bothered by incipient feminist concerns, is that including the feminine range of imagery allows us to keep in place in the doctrine of the Trinity the Genesis teaching that human beings were made in the image of God, 'male and female'.

All three Persons of the Trinity can be styled in the imagery of the human masculine and of the human feminine. But better still, the play of gendered imagery keeps in place the symbols of desire, fecundity, and parental love, while destabilizing any over-literalistic reading. This seems to be the implicit strategy of the Old Testament itself, where images of God as bridegroom and father jostle against one another in a way that would make an overly literalistic reading noxious. A striking medieval example of the same general strategy can be found in Julian of Norwich. So much has been made of Julian's dramatic styling of Christ as mother that we almost fail to notice the splendour of *Revelations of Divine Love* as a piece of Trinitarian theology. I will deal with this at length in the next chapter; here I only wish to point out how confidently Julian sports with threefold titles throughout. In placing great emphasis on Christ as our Mother, she is at once provocative and altogether orthodox: Jesus was indubitably male, yet, if he is to be the perfection of our humanity, he must also be the perfection of female humanity.

---

[31] Ibid. 127.

She is willing to style all three Persons as Mother ('As truly as God is our Father, so truly is God our Mother, and he revealed that in everything, and especially in these sweet words, where he says, I am he, the power and goodness of fatherhood; I am he, the wisdom and the lovingness of motherhood; I am he, the light and grace which is all blessed love').[32]

Julian follows the route not of displacement but of excess, complementing the gendered scriptural terms of divine Fatherhood and Sonship with maternal and functional imagery (God is our Maker, Keeper, and Lover). Yet, just as God can be our Mother as well as our Father, Christ is our Maker as well as our Lover, our Keeper as well as our Maker, the threefold terms revolve in a text which, if effusive, is never careless.

I am suspicious of attempts to purge the Bible's masculine metaphors and 'tidy up' its stories. They veil the historically placed nature of the biblical texts, and are especially misleading if they hope to achieve a theology that is pure, scientific, and free of fable.

In the realm of Trinitarian theology one cannot cease to tell stories, or to remember that they are stories. Athanasius and Augustine are capable of great precision, while at the same time throwing out a profusion of models, or Trinitarian stories—as though they are saying, 'Imagine it is like this, or this, or this...'

Let me then seek not just to comment on previous formulations of the doctrine but also to tell a Trinitarian tale which takes seriously the language of the economy, with all its gendered relational and procreational imagery. As I have already argued,

---

[32] Julian of Norwich, *Showings*, eds. Edmund Colledge and James Walsh (Mahweh, N.J.: Paulist Press, 1978), ch. 59, 295–6.

'father' is a semantically dependent title—it is because there is a child that someone is called a father. It is, in the *technical* sense, a *relational term*. The advent of the child 'gives birth' to the father. In the Christian narrative it is with the Son's death that the distinctive nature of God's fatherhood is established for Christians, for the death of the Son is in some sense also the 'death' of the Father who is one with the Son. Jean-Luc Marion makes a similar suggestion: 'Upon the Cross, the Father expires as much as the Word (Son) since they expire the same Spirit. The Trinity respires from being able to breath among us.'[33] The death of the Son, then, and separation of God from God in the cry of dereliction on the Cross, give way to a new birth, the *ekstasis* which is the mission of the Spirit. It is through the Spirit that there is resurrection and the Church born to newness of life.

The Trinitarian narrative of the economy, in this telling, moves both ways: the Father begets the Son; the Spirit proceeds from the Father and the Son. Yet we can also say that the Son is raised in the Spirit. And the Father *is* Father in virtue of the Son—because it is the child who 'makes' someone a father. The father in this story can no longer have the property, within the economic Trinity, of innascibility (the attribute of being independent of birth) prized by some Trinitarian theologians but predicated only of the Father. In this telling of the economy, the Father, too, 'is born'—or better 'becomes father'—with the Son, and in the Spirit.

This is a vision of a Trinity of complete mutuality, yet it is not one in which all three Persons become the same, as three sides of an equilateral triangle. The First Person, as Unoriginate

---

[33] J-L. Marion, *God without Being* (Chicago: University of Chicago Press, 1991), 142–3.

Origin, begets the Son (is thus named 'Father' by this Son), and from these two proceeds the Spirit. The Son, by being Son, is the one who makes God Father/Mother. The Son gives birth to the Church in the Spirit, represented figuratively in the high tradition of Western religious art by the water and the blood flowing from Christ's pierced side on the Cross—birth imagery. The Spirit is the Lord, the Giver of Life, in whom the son is raised in resurrected life.

From the economic point of view, this story has an exitus–reditus structure: Father–Son–Spirit, Spirit–Son–Father, but at the immanent level it is a story of the perichoretic outpouring of love and birth between the three who *are* only in relation one to another. All three Persons, figuratively, give birth—the First Person as Unoriginate Origin begets the Son and gives the Spirit, the Second as Son 'makes' God the Father and 'gives birth' to the Church on the Cross, and the Holy Spirit, the Lord the Giver of Life, animates the Church in the world. The activity of all three can be styled in the procreative imagery of the human feminine and of the human masculine.[34]

[34] Theories of complete mutuality are not unknown in the history of Trinitarian thought, and I am not sure whether this one is another version of those which speak of God as *Patreque*, *Filioque*, and *Spirituque* (*Patreque* indicating that the Son proceeds from the Father and the Spirit, *Filioque* that the Spirit proceeds from the Father and the Son, and *Spirituque* that the Father proceeds from Son and Spirit, and the Son from Father and Spirit). If so, then it may be subject to Catherine La Cugna's criticism in *God for Us*, an extensive defence of the primacy of the economic (soteriological) Trinity over intellectualizing, immanent accounts of God *in se*. Her criticism of a *Patreque*, *Filioque*, *Spirituque* account (at least as deployed by Leonardo Boff) was that it outstripped anything we know of the economy of salvation and as such is, she says, 'an extreme version of scholastic trinitarian theology' (not a criticism one thinks is usual for Boff) with a 'highly reified account of divine substance'. See C. M. La Cugna, *God for Us: The Trinity and Christian Life* (San Francisco: HarperSanFrancisco, 1991), 277. I am not so sure. Indeed, I am not so sure that scholastic Trinitarian theologies *were* remote from the economy of salvation. But in any case, this retelling of the economic

## Trinity and the 'Feminine Other'

If, as Aquinas suggests, 'relation' is the key to the Trinity, and the to-be of God is to-be-related, then the Son cannot *be* what the Son is except by relation to Father and the Spirit, and the Spirit cannot *be* what the Spirit is except by relation to the Son and the Father, and the Father cannot *be* what the Father is except by relation to the Son and the Spirit. As many classical theologians point out, God is not called 'Father' because he is our father—rather, it is because God is 'Father' to the Son that we are able to pray, 'Our Father'.

The divine Persons cannot be thought of as separate from one another. This full integration of the Holy Spirit, the Lord, the Giver of Life, would go a long way to rectify treatments in which the Spirit does indeed seem, in Elizabeth Johnson's phrase, to be no more than an 'edifying' (perhaps female) 'appendage' to the self-absorbed life of the Father and the Son, the One and the Other, exhausted in their dualism.

The criticisms of Western metaphysics that I discussed earlier are critiques of a philosophy governed by inexorable dualisms, economies of the One and the Same. This, I hazard, could never be a Christian metaphysics, although it might be a particular Neoplatonic heresy. It could only be a metaphysics forgetful of the great efforts made by theologians and philosophers to give account of God's Being as *to-be-related*. We may now stand at a moment of evangelical opportunity in the West, a time in which Christians not only need to hear a fully relational account of the Trinitarian life of God, but may also be receptive to it.

narrative seems to fit the biblical witness and imagery quite well—indeed, it draws our attention, in a way that is not sentimental, to the extensive and hugely neglected repertoire of birth images in the New Testament, often associated with the Spirit. Might not the theological neglect of this birth imagery and the persisting inability to a find proper place for the Spirit in so much modern theology be connected?

We frequently read in the texts of modern theology that we need the doctrine of the Trinity in order to teach us how to be relational beings—a kind of utilitarian apologetics which implies that, while the doctrine doesn't *mean* much any more, it is at least morally useful. But what does the Trinity tell us of human relational experiences? Something has gone seriously wrong if theologians can even ask that kind of question. The sense in which I am here discussing 'relation' in the Trinity is a *formal one*. To give a mundane example, a man becomes a father in a technical sense when he has a child. Even were he to have no idea of the child's existence and thus no 'relationship' (in the vernacular sense) with it, he would nonetheless be related to this child as father. 'Relation' is a useful technical term in Trinitarian theology, and the water is muddied if we forget the several senses, including the modern psychological ones, in which the term can be used.[35]

I was then surprised to find Walter Kasper drawing the following contrast between God and us: whereas God *is* relational, we human beings only *choose* to be relational. He adds, 'relations are essential only to the full self-realisation of the being. A human being is, and remains a human being, even if he selfishly closes himself against relations with others.'[36] What can this mean? Surely we need other human beings, notably parents, to come into being at all. Which human being is free of human relations? As infants, we are entirely dependent on others for our existence. Those others teach us language, values, stories—in short, a world. Even our very limited capacity to 'close ourselves off from others' is conceivable only because

---

[35] This does not mean, of course, that God cannot 'relate to us', in the vernacular sense of the term 'relate'.

[36] W. Kasper, *The God of Jesus Christ* (London: SCM, 1984), 280.

we have *already* been socially constituted. I need other people *even* in order to shut myself off from them. We are constituted, not 'auto-nomously', not despite others, but because of and by others. The more we are 'in relation', the more we are likely to be our selves.[37] We *are* relational beings, and if this is not obvious to us, then it only shows how deeply we are prey to that most insidious of modern myths, the myth of the self-constituting subject of so much modern thought. Human being, like human knowing, not only is not, but could not be, self-constituting.

Is it then a coincidence that the period between the sixteenth and twentieth centuries in the West—a 'Cartesian period', a period which Lacan has called the 'ego's era'—should be both one which has seen a precipitate decline in religious practice in the West and also one in which the affirmation of God as Trinity has again and again been challenged by theologians of deistic, rationalist, or empiricist bent? We could even dare to say that the popular image of God in the mind of many faithful Christians is deistic and Unitarian—the God who is One, and who perhaps has a very special friend, his messenger Jesus, who was sent to make things better for us.

Secular feminism generally is not of the opinion that 'God' has been very good for women, but the 'God' one finds in their texts is a bit player who appears merely as a pretext for the authority of Man and men, the divine guarantor of the veracity of the insights of the Cartesian subject. This 'cogito', self-engendered through denial of the other, the external world, even his own physicality, speaks in the place of and with the authority of 'God'. Rational 'man', viewing things from a

---

[37] This is one of the main thrusts of Taylor's *Sources of the Self*.

'God's-eye view' separates self from other, but there is never any genuine other, always just the 'economy of the Same'. The theologian might object—should object—that this 'God' is not the God of Jesus Christ. This 'God' is a philosophical fiction created by 'Man' for men's purposes, the *'causa sui'*. At most, this 'God' is a binity where in the Second Person is not Jesus but 'Man' himself. Indeed, 'Man' is the senior partner in this idolatrous pair, positing 'God' as the other self to whom he can relate.[38] This is indeed a culture of narcissism where the One (Man) gazes on the other he has made (God made in man's image).[39]

The criticism of this idolatrous God of philosophy is at the heart of Jean-Luc Marion's *God without Being* and also of Heidegger's criticisms of the 'onto-theological constitution of metaphysics' which Marion follows. The God of modern philosophy is *causa sui*, but, as Heidegger says, therefore only an idol before which we can neither pray nor dance.[40] He rightly says that this 'God can come into philosophy only insofar as philosophy... requires or determines that and how God enters into it'.[41] But this is because this is not the true God; this 'God' is a precept of philosophy. Christians do not know God as *causa sui*, but as the God who reveals, as the Gift given.[42]

The Christian doctrine of the Trinity has always been a challenge to philosophies of the One, in both their ancient and their modern forms. The Trinitarian theology of the Cappadocians

---

[38] See La Cugna, *God for Us*, 251.

[39] Rosi Braidotti says, with more truth than she perhaps knows, that this 'God himself is not an infinite Being, for the "I" has accorded to him this essence and his existence, according to the order of Reason' (*Patterns of Dissonance*, 255).

[40] Heidegger, *Identity and Difference*, cited by Marion, *God without Being*, 35.

[41] Ibid. 34.

[42] Marion, *God without Being*, 36.

was formulated over and against just such a metaphysics of the One that contemporary philosophers find so oppressive. The name 'Father', the Cappadocians insisted, does not describe some kind of divine *ousia*, but a relation to the Son.[43] Indeed, if God's 'to be' is 'to-be-related', then all our most seemingly substantive and static divine titles, including those of Father and Son, are really relational. Even to call the First Person 'Unoriginate Origin' is to indicate a relation to that which *is* originated or begotten. Trinitarian theology presents us with a God who cannot be possessed conceptually, but who is totally present to us, as totally Other. Paradoxically, it is with such thoughts that this very Christian doctrine of God's otherness and nearness, the Known Unknowable, to speak in Barthian terms, that one feels also a closeness with our Jewish brothers and sisters. It is not surprising that some of the most productive current thought on a God who 'relates in and through difference' should come from a Jew.[44]

Let us return to de Beauvoir and her well-founded fears for the 'feminine other'. 'No group', she says, 'ever sets itself up as the One without at once setting up the Other over and against itself.'[45] These words sound bitterly across the history of religious sectarianism. Again, de Beauvoir: 'it is not the Other, who, in defining himself as Other, establishes the One. The Other is posed as such by the One in defining himself as the One.'[46] But, according to the doctrine of the Trinity, this is precisely what God does, what God *is*: it is through *being-to-other*, being related, that God is one.

[43] La Cugna, *God for Us*, 66.
[44] See Morny Joy, 'Levinas: Alterity, the Feminine, and Women', *Studies in Religion/Sciences Religieuse*, 22/4 (1993), 463–85.
[45] De Beauvoir, *Second Sex*, 17.     [46] Ibid. 18.

## Trinity and the 'Feminine Other'

The doctrine of the Trinity tells us nothing about how men and women should relate to one another as males and females. It does not show that all men should be like the 'father' and all women model themselves on a feminized Spirit. In this sense the doctrine tells us nothing about sexual difference. But it does let us glimpse what it is, most truly, to be: 'to-be' most fully is 'to-be-related' in difference.

# 7

# The Kindness of God: Trinity and the Image of God in Julian of Norwich and Augustine

O<small>N</small> the face of it, no two texts could be more dissimilar than Augustine's *De Trinitate* and Julian of Norwich's *The Revelation of Divine Love*, or *Shewings*, as it is sometimes called, the first knotty with qualifications and distinctions, the other an outpouring of late medieval piety. The *De Trinitate* is abstract and speculative, while the *Shewings* is a narrative that begins in most particular circumstances, at what Julian believed to be the hour of her death. But neither text is quite what it seems.

Julian's book makes uncomfortable reading in a world unaccustomed to visions. The graphic description of the scourged and blood-soaked Christ with which her *Revelation* opens is so startling as to conceal from us the fact that, as it proceeds, Julian's book is far from merely gruesome, but rather a deeply considered essay on the doctrine of the Trinity (of which she displays a profound and sure-footed knowledge), and on the human predicament.

*The Revelation of Divine Love*, had an uneven reception from the outset, becoming an object of suspicion to church authorities sceptical of women who claimed to have special revelations.

In the seventeenth century, the first in which it was published, Julian's book was vilified by Bishop Stillingfleet as 'the Fantastic Revelations of distempered brains' and the 'blasphemous and senseless tittle tattle' of a gossip.[1] There is now a revival of interest in Julian, not least for her bold descriptions of Christ as mother and her optimism about God's love and forgiveness, so much at odds with the grim, penitential piety of her time.

Stillingfleet, an Anglican bishop little given to 'enthusiasm', could see nothing in the *Revelation* but mystical afflatus, far removed from the twin anchors of Scripture and reason. Today we are better able to appreciate the emotion that Stillingfleet condemned, but it sometimes seems that just in proportion to the book's recovery as a classic of mystical writing, its merit as a work of theology is overlooked. So one hears, as praise, that Julian's book is 'not at all theological', where what is meant is that it is 'from the heart', by contrast with theology's sclerotic pronouncements.

Julian is of a different age, but she is not untheological. What is remarkable about Julian is not so much that she departs from the largely Augustinian orthodoxy of her day, but that she presses it to a new fruitfulness, especially by her unashamed embrace of the body and temporality. Julian's invocation of Christ as mother is justly praised; but to be fully appreciated, it must be seen as the centre-piece of a theology configured by kinship.

I would like in what follows to draw out her ingenuity as a theologian by making a direct comparison of her text with

---

[1] From E. Stillingfleet, *A discourse concerning the idolatry practised in the church of Rome... in answer to some papers of a revolted Protestant* (London: Printed by Robert White for Henry Mortlock, 1672), 224; cited in F. C. Bauerschmidt, *Julian of Norwich and the Mystical Body of Christ* (Notre Dame, Ind.: University of Notre Dame Press, 1999), 1.

Augustine's *de Trinitate*, a work with which it has remarkable, if not immediately evident, similarities of substance, style, and spiritual intent. But first an apology. Reading about Dante is far less satisfactory than reading Dante, and the same is true of Julian. Her short masterpiece, if it could be adequately portrayed in a discursive essay, would not be so great a work of art. It should be read.[2]

## JULIAN'S LITTLE BOOK

Julian's showings have come to us in only a handful of manuscripts, which provide us two versions both evidently her own work. Neither version is raw reportage. Julian is skilful in arranging her materials for greatest impact and her own pastoral purpose, which is to share with her fellow Christians this disclosure of the unstinting love of God.[3]

The circumstances of Julian's showings are given with brevity and clarity at the beginning of her book. On 8 May 1373, Julian lay near to death from an unspecified complaint which numbed her from the waist downward. The parish priest was sent for to give her the last rites, and Julian, accepting the inevitability of death, asked those tending her if she might be propped sitting up with her eyes fixed heavenward, 'where I trusted that I by God's mercy was going'. On arrival, the priest had a different idea.

---

[2] Edmund Colledge, OSA, and James Walsh, SJ, have produced an extremely useful edition in the Classics of Western Spirituality series, which includes both the short and the long text: *Julian of Norwich: Showings* (Mahwah, NJ: Paulist Press, 1978). Much benefit will be derived from reading the book in the Middle English; see *The Showings of Julian of Norwich*, ed. Denise Baker, Norton Critical Edition (New York: W. W. Norton & Company, 2005).

[3] All references are to her long text, unless otherwise indicated.

Holding a crucifix before her face, he said, 'I have brought the image of your saviour; look at it and take comfort from it.' Julian tells us that she privately thought that what she *had* been doing, looking up, was 'good enough'. But she complied with his request, not least because she reckoned she could look straight ahead longer than she could look up, and lowered her gaze to look straight upon the crucifix. There then began a revelation of divine love, a single vision that came to her in sixteen 'showings'.

She recovered, and over the next two decades, living as a solitary (a 'recluse at Norwyche' in the east of England), produced a work now recognized to be in sophistication an achievement on a par with those of Chaucer, her contemporary. It is, as far as we know, the first book written by a woman in English.

Echoes of Augustine are everywhere to be found. 'Our hearts are restless until they rest in thee' becomes in Julian, 'it please him that we should rest in him; for everything which is beneath him is not sufficient for us' (§5).[4] But the similarities go far beyond the adaptation of Augustine's well-known sayings.

We have, it needs to be said, no means of knowing if Julian had herself read Augustine, or even how well and what she could read. So little is known biographically about Julian apart from her text, that we cannot even be sure if 'Julian' was her name. She describes herself as unlearned, but that may mean only that she could not read Latin, or perhaps no more than the Latin of her Vulgate Bible.

However, Julian need not have read Augustine to be Augustinian in her time. It was the orthodoxy. Augustinian friars lived

---

[4] Compare also §56: 'And so I saw most surely that it is quicker for us to come to the knowledge of God than it is to know our own soul. For our soul is so deeply grounded in God and so endlessly treasured that we cannot come to knowledge of it until we first have knowledge of God, who is the Creator to whom it is united.' This is a good summary of the project of Augustine's *Confessions*.

near her in Norwich, and contemporary sermons and spiritual writings were suffused with Augustinian teachings. Elements of *De Trinitate* were well known through Peter Lombard's *Sentences*, which her advisors certainly would have known.[5]

But if Augustine's *De Trinitate* was the standard text on the Trinity for medieval theology, it was not always well understood. Many then, as now, were confused by its apparent lack of system: fifteen books in all, with the first seven expounding the doctrine of the Trinity and, after a transitional book, a final seven devoted to a highly cerebral tour of the way in which the human being is in the image of God, which—according to Augustine—is in the activity of our minds. The last seven books especially have been criticized as rambling and repetitive, and since the Middle Ages the work has been read as virtually two separate treatises, with theologians happy to mine the first seven books for Trinitarian distinctions and leave the later books alone as a recondite exercise in psychology or philosophy of mind.[6]

Augustine himself may have encouraged the impression that *De Trinitate* was a disorganized warren of argument, for in its preface he tells us that it was written during his busy years as a bishop, and that parts of it were smuggled out from under his pen before final editing, which put pressure on him to finish

[5] On this see J. P. H. Clark, 'Time and Eternity in Julian of Norwich', *Downside Review*, 109 (1991), 109. Thomas Aquinas makes use of *De Trinitate*, and Anselm made use of it in both the *Monologion* and the *Proslogion*.

[6] Theological psychology, that is. An extreme and recent example of diremptive misreading is to be found in the Cambridge Political Texts series edition, Augustine, *On the Trinity*, ed. G. B. Matthews *et al.* (Cambridge: Cambridge University Press, 2002), which not only prints only books VIII–XV but introduces these as an essay in the philosophy of mind. One *might* read these books in that way, but it is certain that it is not how Augustine wrote them or intended them to be read. Reading the two halves as essays in first faith and then reason is also anachronistic, imposing a medieval distinction alien to Augustine's own thought.

the rest. But whatever infelicities he might have ironed out had time been given to him, overall structure is not the result of haste but a matter of deliberate intent. Augustine tells us that his 'inquiry proceeds in a closely knit development' from the first of the books to the last, which is why he wanted them read as a whole. Augustine is, after all, attempting to illuminate a mystery with a mystery—to explain God's being (which on his account we cannot know) through our own being, which we also do not understand. His authority for this is Scripture: man is made in the image of God. The image of the Christian God must be triune, and hence the natural affinity of the doctrines of the Trinity with the *imago Dei*, the two halves of his work. It would be surprising if the matter were clear-cut.[7]

It seems that he intended the later books, which can appear meandering, as spiritual exercise. The object of the successive 'psychological' triads, culminating in memory, understanding, and will, was not to prove that man, by these faculties, mirrors the divine being, but a textual strategy by which we might come to know ourselves as remembering God, understanding God, and willing God, and thus be open to becoming what God intends us to be.[8]

---

[7] Compare Etienne Gilson: 'What a man finds *circa se* or *sub se* is overwhelming in amount, what he finds *in se* is embarrassing in its obscurity, but when from his own being he would obtain light as to what is *supra se*, then indeed he finds himself face to face with a dark and somewhat terrifying mystery. The trouble is that he is himself involved in the mystery. If, in any true sense, man is an image of God, how should he know himself without knowing God? But if it is really *of God* that he in an image, how should he know himself?' (*The Spirit of Medieval Philosophy* (New York: Charles Scribners Sons, 1940), 219).

[8] On *De Trinitate* and spiritual exercise see L. Ayres, 'The Christological Context of Augustine's *de Trinitate* XIII: Toward Relocating Books VIII–XV', *Augustinian Studies*, 29 (1998), 111–39.

Julian, remarkably, treats together precisely the two doctrines which most medieval theologians, despite their indebtedness to *De Trinitate*, separated: the doctrine of the Trinity and the doctrine of *imago Dei*. Taking these doctrines together is one similarity of the two works. Another is that Julian's 'ramblings', like those of *De Trinitate's* last books, are now thought to be considered and deliberate. Neither work is intended simply as exposition; both present an inward drama which the reader is invited to perform and re-create. Julian explains her intention at the outset, saying that she saw from her first showing that God 'clothes' us in himself and 'enfolds' us in his love. Her prose seeks to do the same, 'folding' the reader into its purposes in a manner that anticipates the fugal treatment of the Trinity in Karl Barth's *Church Dogmatics*. Like *De Trinitate*, Julian's is a text which aims not just 'to tell about' something, but to recruit the reader as fellow traveller into the mystery of the love of God—hence its distinctive recursive style.[9]

So there are these similarities of form between Julian and Augustine: the wedding of the doctrine of the Trinity with that of *imago Dei* and the recursive style. In the matter of content, both are concerned with the Trinity and with our union with the God of love. Yet Julian's *Shewings* cannot but strike the reader as homely and comfortable in a way that Augustine's *De Trinitate* is not: while her central metaphors are drawn from family life—birth, gestation, growth, and kinship—his are drawn from mental activity—choosing, willing, remembering, understanding, all of which heighten the 'disembodied' feeling of his book by contrast with the almost tactile atmosphere of

---

[9] See Baker, *Julian of Norwich's Showings*, for a discussion of the recursive structure of the book.

Julian's. And this comes down to where, respectively, they wish to lodge the image of God in humankind.

For Augustine, as has been mentioned, it is by virtue of our mind or inner self (*mens*) that we are in the image of God. This was a favoured view at his time, for certainly God does not have a body, and any crudely physical imaging of the divine would seem out of the question. Augustine develops this *intellectualist* interpretation, pressing home its advantages. It allows him to say that women are as fully *in the image* as men, since they share the same minds. It spurs him on to find 'threefoldnesses' in mental life. It enables him to insist that each person is fully in the image of the Triune God, and not as a member of a team of three, like the domestic triad of father, mother, and child. After traversing a number of mental analogies, Augustine settles on memory, understanding, and will as most adequately reflecting the divine life. More precisely, it is in the *activities* of remembering, understanding, and willing or loving (these last here interchangeable), and supremely in remembering, understanding, and loving 'him by which it was made' (xiv. 12. 15) that the inner self is most God-like.[10]

This 'intellectualist' understanding of the *imago Dei* as developed by Augustine became dominant in Western theology. But along with advantages come limitations: most notably, what on this account is to become of the body? Does the body play no

[10] Edmund Hill, OP, in introducing his translation of *De Trinitate*, points out that Peter Lombard disastrously misunderstood Augustine by taking him to speak of three 'faculties' of the soul—memory, understanding, and will. However, in Augustine these are not mental faculties but mental activities, and part of the unfolding history of the self. Thomas Aquinas corrected Lombard, but his corrective was not always remarked (Augustine, *The Trinity*, ed. E. Hill *et al.* (New York: New City Press [for the] Augustinian Heritage Institute, 1990), 'Introduction', 26). See also, along the same lines, R. Williams, '*Sapientia* and the Trinity'.

part in the human image of God? Bernard McGinn, summarizing the contributions of the intellectualist approach through the twelfth century, says that the

limitations of traditional *imago Dei* anthropology and the ascetical and mystical programs to which it gave rise have become obvious with the passage of time. The concentration on the soul, or inner person, as the true image and the difficulties that thinkers in this tradition had in expressing the substantial union of the body and soul led to systematic ambiguities that encouraged depreciation of the body and sometimes skewed the sanity of ascetical observances.[11]

In this loss of the body, the female body was particularly at risk, being mired in birth and child-rearing and far from the soaring life of the soul; and this is not assisted by Augustine's linking, in *De Trinitate*, of the feminine with lower and bodily activity, a point to which I will return.[12] Augustine consistently privileged mind over body, sometimes identifying the self with mind alone, and sometimes speaking of the mind as *using* the body.[13]

---

[11] B. McGinn, (1987). 'The Human Person as Image of God: Western Christianity', in B. McGinn and J. Meyendorff (eds.), *Christian Spirituality* (New York: Crossroad; London: SCM, 1985), 312–30, at 328.

[12] Cf. Rowan Williams: 'As has more than once been remarked Augustine is not the first to conceive the will to know God in strongly affective or erotic terms: Plotinus bequeathed to him the language of *eros* towards the One, and the earlier Augustine had frequently taken this language, as a Neoplatonist well might, to entail the rejection of goods other than the One, and a desire to leave behind time, body and passion' ('The Paradoxes of Self-Knowledge in Augustine's *De trinitate*', in J. Lienhard, SJ, Earl Muller, SJ, and Roland Teske, SJ (eds.), *Augustine Presbyter Factus Sum* (New York: Peter Lang, 1993), 132–3.

[13] See Augustine, *Confessions*, x. xvii. 26: 'And this mind, this is I myself. What then am I, my God?' On this issue, and for Augustine's oscillations on mind and body, see G. Lawless, *Augustine and Human Embodiment*, in *Collectanea Augustiniania* (Louvain: Leuven University Press, 1999), 167–86. This discomfort with the body was a feature of the Christian Platonism of Ambrose, with its flight from the world.

The Christological difficulty with this privileging of mind over body lies with its implications for the doctrine of the Incarnation; for if our human object is to flee from bodiliness and temporality, then why did God embrace both states in becoming man? Augustine is aware of this tension, but even as late as *de Trinitate* is struggling to overcome it, still exalting the eternal and unchanging over the temporal and contingent, as we can see in book XII, where Augustine sets himself the task of explaining why St Paul appears to attribute the image of God to the man only, and not to the woman.

## BOOK XII: SAVING PAUL

It is hard not to feel sorry for Augustine as he tries to reconcile two apparently conflicting biblical claims while insisting that both are entirely correct: Gen. 1: 27 and 1 Cor. 11: 7 ('For a man ought not to have his head veiled, since he is the image and reflection of God, but woman is the reflection of man'). According to Augustine, St Paul *cannot* mean that women are not 'in the image of God', since Genesis so clearly says they are. Paul must therefore be speaking *symbolically*, and since the *imago Dei* is found in the mind, he is speaking about mind or reason. Drawing on pagan philosophical divisions of the mind into 'higher' contemplative functions and 'lower' practical ones, Augustine argues that Paul is distinguishing that part of the mind which contemplates eternal truth from the part which is 'drawn off from it and assigned and directed to the management of temporal affairs' (XII. 10). Paul (according to Augustine) symbolizes them as male and female—the 'male' of the mind 'adheres to eternal ideas to contemplate or consult them', and the 'female' of the mind acts, Eve-like, as a helper by taking care of the necessities of life. Just as in married union male and female are two in one flesh (Gen. 2: 24), so these higher and lower activities are embraced in every mind.

Augustine was clearly satisfied with this reading of Paul, which appears as early as the *Confessions* and endures through to *De Trinitate*. It follows that women can contemplate the eternal things as well as men, since every mind has these higher and lower ('male' and 'female') aspects, *sapientia* (wisdom) and *scientia* (knowledge) respectively. But it is only in the sapiential aspect of mind (that marked 'male') that we find the image of God.

Treating male and female as symbolic markers for human traits did not begin with Augustine. Pagan and Jewish writers had done so, and Ambrose, Augustine's mentor, had produced allegorical interpretations of Genesis in which Eve was symbolically 'the senses of the body' which lead Adam (reason) to stray. Augustine refers to these interpretations, and criticizes them—'I did not think the woman should be made to stand for the senses of the body which we observe to be common to us and to the beasts' (XII. 19). His own interpretation is an improvement, he believes, because both male and female signify reason, but of two different sorts—practical and contemplative. This he finds apt, because (patterning his comments after the narrative of the creation of Eve in Genesis) that part of our mind which consults 'highest and innermost truth' (*sapientia*) could find no partner or helper in those qualities it shares with beasts. Instead, part of the mind is 'derived' or taken away (*scientia*), like the spare rib, to help in the matter of temporal things: getting dressed in the morning, feeding ourselves, raising children, working at our jobs. But it is by the renewal of spirit of our minds (here intending its higher, sapiential function) that we are made heirs to grace,

And it is according to this renewal, also, that we are made sons of God by the baptism of Christ; and putting on the new man...who is there, then, who will hold women to be alien from this fellowship, whereas they are fellow-heirs of grace with us ? (xii. 7).[14]

The integrity of Scripture is maintained; women are fully in the image of God (albeit through the 'male' of their minds), and Paul is reconciled with Genesis. But Augustine has created other problems with these symbolic callisthenics. The problem is rather that the whole realm of the transient and everyday—of suppers cooked, noses wiped, gardens dug, sick tended, risks becoming a mere staging post in the soul's ascent to a higher wisdom.

No orthodox theologian can condemn outright our bodily nature, but Augustine never quite escapes distrust of the body and its temptations.[15] In his early works especially, the temporal and contingent, the things of the body, are a drag on the mind, which seeks the eternal. Perfection in Christian life is a matter of *ascent* to a higher realm, and where spiritual progress is mapped on the vertical, a hierarchy of value is usually implied. Thus, in the early *De vera Religione* Augustine, explaining the loss inflicted by original sin, does so by listing a series of the 'good' and the 'less good': Adam and Eve expelled

[14] Augustine is thinking of Eph. 4: 22–4: 'You were taught to put away your former way of life, your old self, corrupt and deluded by its lusts, and to be renewed the spirit of your minds, and to clothe yourselves with the new self, created according to the likeness of God in true righteousness and holiness.' Both men and women are re-created to this likeness.

[15] Andrew Louth has noted that a 'sense of not being at home in the world is fundamental to Augustine's mystical thought' (*The Origins of the Christian Mystical Tradition: From Plato to Denys* (Oxford: Oxford University Press, 1981), 134).

from Paradise pass 'not from substantial good to substantial evil, for there is no substantial evil—but from eternal good to temporal good, from spiritual to carnal good, from intelligible to sensible good, from the highest to the lowest good'.[16] They have not moved off the ladder of divine providence, but down it. Adam's transgression must be, for Augustine, 'a fall', since its remedy is 'an ascent'.[17] Even in the maturity of *De Trinitate* we find him saying that 'too many advances into this lower territory' (*scientia*) distract the mind from contemplating truth (XII.10). The body continues to be a nuisance, and the inability to control the movements of the genitalia, even when not required for procreation, is a sign that we are far from the *apatheia* that Adam and Eve would have known in Paradise.[18]

---

[16] *De vera Religione*, 38, cited by C. Harrison, *Beauty and Revelation in the Thought of Saint Augustine* (Oxford: Clarendon Press, 1992), 42. Harrison adds that 'corporeal beauty is described as the "lowest beauty" but this is likewise not to imply that it is "deceptive" or "evil", but simply to warn that when man regards it—"the beauty of the sky, the order to the stars, the brightness of the light"—he should not treat the "number", "form", or "measure" he finds there with curiosity or pride, but, Augustine comments, "a step should be taken towards immortal things that abide forever"'.

[17] In an article which emphasizes Augustine's high regard for the body, George Lawless nonetheless acknowledges that 'Augustine's view of reality never parts company completely with the vertical structure of higher and lower goods, more important and less important values, different levels of beauty alongside a concomitant hierarchy of truths—all of which he inherited and modified appreciably from the Platonic insistence upon participation in degrees or grades of being. There remains throughout Augustine's eventful life a propensity to heighten or to overestimate the importance of the soul at the possible expense of the body' (*Augustine and Human Embodiment*, 173).

[18] 'For while it is true that the carnal desire dwelling in the genital organs is made good use of by married chastity, still it has its involuntary motions which show that either it could not have been present at all in paradise before sin, or if it did exist there that it was not such as would ever resist the will. But now our experience of it is that it *fights against the law of the mind* (Rom. 7.23), and even when it is not required for procreation it goads us on to copulation; if we give in it is sated by sinning, if we do not give in it is curbed by refusal; both situations which no one can doubt were foreign to paradise before sin' (*De Trinitate*, XIII. 23).

In book XII, as we have seen, the relation of wisdom to knowledge is still the relation of higher to lower, and symbolically of male to female. *Sapientia* and *scientia* together make up the mind, but only in the higher of the two, *sapientia*, will we find the image of God. Augustine is patronizing about the knowledge of temporal things, which 'is good within its proper limits' and, as long as it is not puffed up, is indeed necessary for the life of virtue. But 'knowledge' (the way 'we make good use of temporal things') is lower than 'the contemplation of eternal things', or wisdom (XII. 4). In a formula for the spiritual life that goes back in Greek philosophy at least to Plutarch, we progress through the things of this world to contemplation of the divine.

This is all in sharp contrast to spiritual life as we find it in the *Revelation of Divine Love*. While Augustine calls us up into the mind, Julian immerses herself in the body. This is no less than Augustine's *De Trinitate* an exploration of the *imago Dei*, and no less biblically inspired, for Julian has chosen to privilege, not Genesis 1, but the numerous New Testament texts where Jesus is said to be the true image of the invisible God. It is entirely relevant that her showings begin with bodies, her own ailing body and the distressed body of Christ.

## THE FIRST SHOWING

Since all sixteen showings flow from the first, it is well to attend to it closely. Immediately her parish priest held the crucifix before her, she saw the head of Christ: 'And at this, suddenly I saw the red blood running down from under the crown, hot and flowing freely and copiously, a living stream, just as it was at the time when the crown of thorns was pressed on his blessed head' (§4).

Julian's was an age deeply interested in the body, and especially the wounded body of Christ on the cross, evident in art and observance. The recovery of Aristotle by Aquinas in the thirteenth century brought a new affirmation of the physical to theology, and by the late fourteenth century doleful meditations on the wounds of Christ had become something of a cliché of popular piety—a cliché which Julian seems content to repeat. But, as David Aers points out, she 'only seems' to do so.

The grett droppes of blode felle downe fro under the garlonde lyke pellotes semyng as it had comynn oute of the veynes... The plentuoushede is lyke to the droppes of water that falle of the eveysyng of an howse after a grete shower of reyne that falle so thycke that no man may nomber them with no bodely wyt. And for the roundnesse they were lyke to the scale of heryng in the spredyng, the droppes of the evesyng of a howse for the plentuoushede unnumerable (§7).

Although beginning with the stricken Christ, whose sufferings are brought from the past into the immediate present, Julian does not proceed with a series of heart-wrenching reflections on pains and piercings; nor does she involve us in the sufferings of Mary or the others at the foot of the Cross. Instead Julian turns almost at once to the doctrine of the Trinity, normally considered one of Christianity's most abstruse teachings.[19] Julian tells us that even while the crucified

---

[19] See David Aers, 'The Humanity of Christ', in Baker, *Julian of Norwich's Showings*, 160. Aers says: 'What happens here is that the kind of elaborations encouraged by the dominant forms of devotion of Christ's humanity and passion are not delivered. Indeed they are positively blocked off as the familiar images are turned into theological reflections on the Trinity.'

Christ was before her eyes, the Trinity filled her with the greatest joy: 'For Trinity is God, God is the Trinity. The Trinity is our maker, the Trinity is our protector, the Trinity is our everlasting lover, the Trinity is our endless joy and our bliss, by our Lord Jesus Christ and in our Lord Jesus Christ' (§4); for, says Julian (adding an important interpretive principle), 'where Jesus appears the blessed Trinity is always understood, as I see it'.

Next the Virgin Mary comes to her mind as barely more than a girl. Julian marvels that the Creator should be born of his own creature. She is shown 'a spiritual sight of his familiar love': God clothes us in his love. Her language is physical, and echoes the clothing of God in flesh in the Virgin's womb to which she has just alluded. Now God 'is our clothing, who wraps and enfolds us for love, embraces us and shelters us, surrounds us for love, which is so tender that he may never desert us' (§5). In the next moment Julian passes to a cosmic vision of all that is made, seen to her inward sight as small and round as a hazel nut cupped in the palm of her hand.[20] She marvels that something so small (all that is) does not just disintegrate; but her mind supplies the answer: 'It lasts and always will because God loves it' (§5). Although Julian does not name it as such, this is her exposition of creation *ex nihilo*: such a fragile world might suggest a distant, fearsome, and overbearing God, but in Julian's text the opposite is the case—the very precariousness of the world underscores the extent to which God loves it. Were God to cease loving the world for an instant, it would simply slip out of existence. Instead, not

[20] It is worth noting that she sees 'all that is' as a little ball in the palm of *her* hand, not in that of God, as is sometimes mistakenly said. The emphasis is on the fragility of creation, not God's 'bigness'.

only is God wholly good, but what God made is good. Evil can have no real existence as something over and against the good. It can only be privative—a lack. This is Augustinian, and it is hard to see what other conclusion one could come to, having thought through the implications of creation *ex nihilo*. 'Wickedness' can only have the status of being tolerated. It has no being in its own right.[21]

The vision of the fragility of creation bears the inference that God sustains in love each thing in particular, and this forms a way back to the particularity of the bloodied face of Christ on the cross, to which she returns at the end of her account of the first showing, saying that all the time she saw these things with her inward sight, her actual eyes had continually before them the bleeding head of Christ. From these interlocking elements of the first showing, the whole of Julian's subsequent theological vision unfolds.

Julian came to see this first showing with its sustained vision of Christ on the cross as pointing to a profound theological truth: our way to God is only through the Word made flesh. She will look nowhere else than to the Incarnate Lord. Prompted later in the showings to look away from the Cross and up to heaven to the Father, she makes an inward reply, 'No, I cannot, for you are my heaven' (§19).[22] Chapter 6 explains why: the chief means that God has ordained to help us is 'the blessed

---

[21] Compare Augustine: 'As for the way in which man was handed over into the devil's power, this should not be thought of as though God actually did it or ordered it to be done, but merely that he permitted it, albeit justly' (*De Trinitate*, XIII. 16; ed. Hill, 355).

[22] The wider context is this: 'I saw clearly by the faith I had that there was nothing between the cross and heaven to distress me. I had either to look up or to reply. So I made inward answer as firmly as I could, and said, "No. I cannot. You are my heaven"' (§19).

nature which he took of the virgin'.[23] This translation loses something of the Middle English, which reads 'that blessed *kynde* that he toke of the maiden' (my italics). Christ is 'our kind', a human being like us, and by extension 'our kin'. Clothed in human flesh in the Virgin's womb, Christ will in turn clothe us in God's love. Julian tells us that just 'as the body is clad in the cloth, and the flesh in the skin, and the bones in the flesh, and the heart in the trunk, so are we, soul and body, clad and enclosed in the goodness of God' (§6). Even more so, for these garments wear out, but God's love never will. Our human bodies, once mapped on Christ's human body, are not obstacles to salvation, but its very means. The Word Incarnate in embracing embodied life blesses its contingent and fragile nature.

Julian believes that God has made us for himself alone, and, as a good Augustinian, says that she will 'never have true rest or happiness' until 'so fastned to him that ther be right nought that is made betweene my God and me' (§5). But how is this to be achieved? For Julian it does not mean escaping the trials of the body or, despite the fact that she lived many years as a recluse, avoiding other people—that would be to flee Christ, her heaven. From her initial vision of creation Julian can see the world only as good, not just in its first creating but even now. Julian implicitly joins Being and Good. Were the world not good, it would not be.[24] Sin may have robbed the world of joy, but it cannot take away its goodness. Change, sorrow, and loss—what Julian calls the 'heavyness and irkehede of our fleshly liveing' (§1)—cannot finally be alien to God's plan of

---

[23] Ch. 6 in the longer version. This chapter is new to the longer version.

[24] 'All our Lord does is right, and what he permits is worthwhile...all that is good is done by our Lord, and all that is evil is permitted by him' (§35).

love, or (as they sometimes seem in Augustine) obstacles to our spiritual progress.

Because 'all that is' is good, Julian takes for granted the necessities which frame our lives—in high winds and storms boats will sink. Human beings, necessitous creatures, in the midst of crops that fail and diseases that ruin the body will grieve and sorrow and rage and sin. God foresees this, but creates us anyway. The 'Fall' in Julian's scheme is not something which happened long ago in Eden for which all men and women are subsequently punished. The 'Fall', or 'falling', happens to every one almost every day, and is the way in which 'man who is to be saved' learns and grows. It is part of the course we run, and were we never to fall, we would never fully appreciate the astonishing love of our Maker.

It is by way of illumining this 'astonishing love' that Julian turns to motherhood. Mothering images appear only late in the longer version of the *Revelation*, after and largely by way of what Julian calls the 'wonderful example' of the Lord and his servant in chapter 51. Here Julian sees a servant, shabbily dressed, standing next to his Lord, who is seated. The Lord sends out the servant, who runs 'in grett hast' to fulfil his master's will, but then falls into a ditch, injuring himself so badly that he is unable to turn to look and see that his Lord loves him. This example is not mentioned in the shorter text, because Julian was unsure of its meaning. After years of reflection, she came to see it as the answer to a troubling difficulty of her vision: why is it, when we are so clearly blameworthy, that she could see no blame or anger in God, no more than 'if we were as pure and holy as the angels are in heaven' (§50)? She now understands that the servant represents Adam and 'everyman', but also Christ. Accordingly, the Lord's loving gaze is both upon fallen Adam and upon Christ. The servant's thread-bare clothing is the human condition.[25] The Lord's gaze on the servant accordingly is binocular, a 'fitting blend of compassion and pity, of joy and blessedness... The compassion and pity was that of the Father when his most loved creation, Adam, fell; the joy and blessedness was in his own beloved Son who is equal with the Father' (§51).

'Mercy' and 'grace' are the divine response to human fallen-ness. God has created humankind 'good', but has destined it to be 'even better' through the workings of mercy and grace. But to know this mercy and grace, we *need* to have fallen. This is Julian's *felix culpa*, for the last state will be better than the first. Just as our own perversity causes pain, so God's grace and forgiveness disclose to us a love such as we would not know, had we not suffered previously.

Our falling is not disastrous. God is not 'angry'. Julian asserts that God 'cannot be angry—that would be impossible'; for if God were to be angry but for a moment, we could not live (§49). Why do we fall? The mother lets the young child slip from her hand, not hoping the child will fall, but knowing that it probably will. She does so because she knows that the child will not learn to walk or run without falling first. 'We need to fall.' That is the divine pedagogy. And we need to know that we need to fall.

This brings us to the kindness of God. Julian's theology of 'at-one-ing', for that is what atonement means, is grounded in the biblical insight that through Christ, believers become the

---

[25] It is likely that behind the example is the Christ hymn in Phil. 2: 6–7, that Christ, 'who, though he was in the form of God, did not regard equality with God as something to be exploited, but emptied himself, taking the form of a slave, being born in human likeness'. This passage is important to the Christology of *De Trinitate*, as well, especially in the first seven books. See, e.g., *De Trinitate*, I. 14–15.

*kin* of Christ, either adoptively or by new birth. Thus Paul to the Ephesians:

Blessed be the God and Father of our Lord Jesus Christ, who has blessed us in Christ with every spiritual blessing in the heavenly places, just as he chose us in Christ before the foundation of the world to be holy and blameless before him in love. He destined us *for adoption as his children* through Jesus Christ, according to the good pleasure of his will, to the praise of his glorious grace that he freely bestowed on us in the Beloved (Eph. 1: 3–6, my italics).

And even more dramatically in Romans:

We know that all things work together for good for those who love God, who are called according to his purpose. For those whom he foreknew he also predestined to be conformed *to the image of his Son*, in order that he might be the firstborn within a large family [firstborn among many brothers]. And those whom he predestined he also called; and those whom he called he also justified; and those whom he justified he also glorified (Rom. 8: 28–30, my italics).[26]

Both passages link kinship with Christ to a love that anticipates our very being, a love from 'before the foundation of the world'. Julian's originality lies in her alignment of Paul's language of atonement as fraternal kinship (Christ, the firstborn of many brothers), with the second birth imagery of the gospels. Yet this association is there for the asking. It is astonishing how few theologians have made anything of this connection of kinship and atonement when birth imagery is plain to read in the New Testament. Nowhere is it more powerful than in the Prologue to John's Gospel:

[26] The Greek reads 'firstborn of many brothers'.

He was in the world, and the world came into being through him; yet the world did not know him. He came to what was his own, and his own people did not accept him. But to all who received him, who believed in his name, he gave power to become the children of God, who were born, not of blood or of the will of the flesh or of the will of man, but of God (John 1: 10–13).

Julian, then, has good biblical warrant for believing that the Second Person of the Trinity is our mother twice over, at our first creating when the world was made ('the world came into being through him' (John 1: 10)) and by our 'second birth' through the Word Incarnate.

Who will be saved? Julian is cautious—perhaps her confessors warned her away from her own vision of an empty hell. But her soteriology is tied to her protology (what God does in creating) and to her eschatology, and she is scarcely more universalist than Paul himself in Colossians when he says that Christ

is the image of the invisible God, the firstborn of all creation; for in him all things in heaven and on earth were created, things visible and invisible, whether thrones or dominions or rulers or powers—all things have been created through him and for him. He himself is before all things, and in him all things hold together. His is the head of the body, the church: he is the beginning, the firstborn from the dead, so that he might come to have the first place in everything. For in him all the fullness of God was pleased to dwell, and through him God was pleased to reconcile to himself all things, whether on earth or in heaven, by making peace through the blood of his cross (Col. 1: 15–20).

Julian's insistence that in every 'man who will be saved' there is some substance which is so knit to God that it 'has never been and never can be separated from him' is not remote from the orthodox claim that the *imago Dei* is never entirely effaced in the human being, but in Julian is heightened by her sense of the kinship of Christ.[27] Julian believes, again quite scripturally, that we are fashioned twice over in the image of God: at our first creating, as described in Genesis ('in the image of God he created them'), and in our new creation in Christ, the very image of the invisible God ('glory as of the only son of the Father').

This provides an interesting contrast with Augustine's procedure in *De Trinitate*. In that book's lengthy treatment of the *imago Dei*, Augustine makes little use of the scriptural passages which speak of Christ as the true image, choosing instead to develop the divine plural of Genesis 1 ('let us make man in our image') and to seek a triune *imago* in every mind.[28] Augustine may have been wary of any suggestion that the human being is made only in the image of the Second Person, thus making an unacceptable distinction between the Persons of the Trinity. Julian leaps over this by simply conflating Genesis and the New Testament, telling us that where she says 'Jesus' she means 'Trinity'.[29] We are made in the triune image at our creating (*pace* Genesis) and remade in the image of God through Jesus Christ. In our second birth bodies are to the fore, both that of Christ and our own bodies, and it is by no mere whim that

[27] 'I saw and understood very surely that in each soul which will be saved there is a godly will which never assented to sin nor ever will' (§53).

[28] In *De Trinitate* xii. 7 he expressly mentions his concern with those who see humankind as being fashioned 'to the image of the Son'. But 'if devout faith teaches, as indeed it does, that the Son is like the Father to the point of being identical in being, then whatever is being made to the likeness of the Son must also be made to the likeness of the Father' (xii. 7). On this see R. A. Markus, '*Imago* and Similitude in Augustine', *Revue des Études Augustiniennes*, 10 (1964), 125–43.

[29] The underpinning for this is the unity of all God's works *ad extra*.

Julian refuses to turn her gaze in any other direction. It is through Christ's body that her own will know God's mercy and grace.

Like Augustine, Julian finds a lower and a higher part to our being—the higher our 'substantial', and the lower our 'sensual' nature. Substance and sensuality together make up the soul (§56) and correspond to Augustine's *wisdom* and *knowledge*; but Julian does not identify them symbolically as 'male' or 'female', nor does she set one above the other. Both 'substantial' and 'sensual' natures are beloved of God, and in both, God is at work: 'I saw that God never began to love mankind,' says Julian,

for just as mankind will be in endless bliss ... just so has that same mankind been known and loved in God's prescience from without beginning in his righteous intent. And by the endless intent and assent and the full accord of the Trinity, the mediator wanted to be the foundation and the head of this fair nature, out of whom we all have come, in whom we are all enclosed, into which we all shall go, finding in him our full heaven in everlasting joy by the prescient purpose of all the blessed Trinity from without beginning. For before he made us he loved us, and when we were made we loved him (§53).

This dense passage repays attention, for here Julian makes the bold move, taken in the twentieth century by Karl Barth, of treating predestination as the predestining of Christ to be the head of human nature, in whom all are included. Christ is our origin and our way to God. He is the head of our 'fair nature, out of whom we all have come, in whom we are all enclosed, into which we all shall go'. The human being is glorious, not lowly, because Christ is glorious; and something similar seems to be true of the human body.

Although there is a lower and a higher nature in Julian, and the 'lower' is sensual, there is no sense that the lower is less regarded than the higher. The Lord himself is at constant work in the lower part of our human nature. While the higher part knows 'great love and marvellous joy' (cf. Augustine's timeless and eternal truths), the lower part knows 'pains and sufferings, compassions and pities, mercies and forgiveness and other such' (§52). These 'are profitable', and none of these would be our lot were we not fallible and fallen. The vigour of the lower part of our nature springs from the higher, and in God's sight there is no difference, for the same love pervades all (§52).

In bold reversal of the theological norm, the problem of the 'two natures' in Julian's theology is not that of Christ's two natures—for he is wonderfully and wholly one—but ours, since it is in the 'sons of Adam' that substantial goodness and sensual nature have sheered apart. 'God is closer to us than our own soul,' says Julian, echoing Augustine but providing her own explanation: 'for he is the foundation on which our soul stands, and he is the mean which keeps the substance and the sensuality together, so that they will never separate' (§56).

Julian's narrative of our earthly pilgrimage in the example of the Lord and the servant is not set out in terms of Neoplatonic ascent of a ladder of perfection. Her metaphor is more nearly horizontal and earthly, for the servant runs *across* the countryside and 'falls', not down a ladder, but into a ditch. She does not set the eternal over the temporal, for she sees that God is at work in both our substantial and our sensual natures, and Christ pre-eminently in the latter.[30] It follows from this that

---

[30] 'I saw with absolute certainty that our substance is in God, and moreover, that he is in our sensuality, too' (§44). Augustine, with his concern not to divide the Trinity, would be pleased to see that Julian says, 'Our essential nature is entire

the Incarnation cannot be simply a rescue operation once things have gone wrong. God has loved humankind since 'before the foundation of the world'. The moment God becomes clothed in human flesh in the womb of Mary marks a triumphant unfolding of God's plan of love. The impatient otherworldliness of Augustinianism, for which the flesh is a drag and a distraction on the soul's journey to the uncreated, is brought firmly down to earth. Why should we desire to flee our physical nature if God has chosen to become our kind?

It is this 'kindness' of God that renders not just motherhood but all kinship metaphors so appropriate when speaking of God. Julian does not confine herself to any one:

Our great Father, almighty God, who is being, knows us and loved us before time began. Out of this knowledge, in his most wonderful deep love, by the prescient eternal counsel of all the blessed Trinity, he wanted the second person to become our Mother, our brother and our saviour. From this it follows that as truly as God is our Father, so truly is God our Mother (§59).

God, or more particularly Christ, is our Mother because his work is not completed at Bethlehem. Julian sees Christ as continually 'in travail', labouring to give birth to humankind in the fullness of its intended being. Our human mothers, whose office is a great one, bear us to pain and death, but Christ—true Mother and 'All-love'—bears us to joy and eternal life. In this divine pregnancy, 'he carries us within him in love and travail, until the full time when he wanted to suffer the sharpest thorns and cruel pains that ever were or will be, and at last he died' (§60).

in each Person of the Trinity, who is one God. Our sensual nature is in the Second Person alone, Jesus Christ' (§58).

In this life, Christ is our fellow traveller. In Julian's Middle English, 'travails' carries three meanings: Christ labours with us (gives birth), sorrows with us (shares our travails), and, in doing both, 'travels' with us on our way.[31] We sorrow and stumble, but Christ is always leading us amidst life's changes and chances. In this way we grow, learning from the 'irkehede' of life of the love of God.[32] This growth is not just of the mind or spirit, for Christ indwells us 'until the time that we are fully grown, our soul together with our body and our body together with our soul' (§55).

Christ, our way and our end, brings us to a bliss we would not know apart from 'travelling' with him. As Christ in life carried his cross, so 'we are therefore in suffering and labour with him as our nature requires' ('therefore we arn in desese and *travel with hym* as our frelete askyth' (§21, my italics)). Each of us must travail. Even the happiest life ends in death, but our travails—our work and struggles, like that of Christ or a woman in labour—are productive pains, struggles to joy and new life.

In the final chapter Julian tells us that, after more than fifteen years pondering the meaning of her showings, she understood that 'love' was her Lord's meaning: 'I saw very certainly that . . . before God made us he loved us, which love was never abated and never will be . . . In our creation we had beginning, but the love in which he created us was in him from without beginning. In this love we have our beginning, and all this shall we see in God without end' (§86).

---

[31] 'Thus he susteyneth us with himselfe in love, and traveled into the full tyme that he wold suffer the sharpist throwes and the grevousest peynes that ever were or ever shall be, and dyed at the last' (§97).

[32] 'And the nature of this blessed love is such that we shall know in God what we should never have known had we not suffered previously' (§58).

Travelling with God may not always be congenial, but it is always a matter of joy for those who know themselves to be on the way. Jesus, 'our true Mother', in taking 'our nature (the takyng of oure kynd) gave us life, and in his blessed dying on the Cross he bore us to endless life. And since that time, now and ever until the day of judgment, he feeds us and fosters us, just as the great supreme lovingness of motherhood wishes, and as the natural need of childhood asks' (§63). Then, says, Julian, we will know the true meaning of the words 'All shall be wele' (§63).

It is tempting to see Julian as casting off gloomy Augustinianism entirely, but she is remarkably faithful to his legacy, while changing his emphasis. Where Augustine sees the cup half empty, she sees it half full; where he looks backwards to the Fall, she looks forward to union with God. *De Trinitate* speaks of our thirst for God, Julian of God's thirst for us.

In the end, the two are not so far apart, especially if we turn our attention to book XIII of *De Trinitate*. Here Augustine continues his discussion of *sapientia* and *scientia* (as in book XII), but his tone has changed. Between completing book XII and beginning book XIII, Augustine had ceased working on the manuscript for several years, 'after tiresome friends had pirated what he had already written'.[33] Augustine is no longer so condescending about the realm of the temporal. He begins the chapter with a close reading of the prologue to John's gospel, dividing it between the graces which come through God's eternal Word and those which come through the agency of the Incarnate Word in time. The Word made flesh must unite temporal and eternal, and indeed, he says, many other

---

[33] Edmund Hill, in a footnote to his translation of *De Trinitate*, 366.

things that the philosophers keep separate. Augustine rehearses many of points which will be made later by Julian. The whole person is not just *mens*, but soul and body, for the body too will know immortality (XIII. 12). Those who doubt Julian's orthodoxy on the matter of divine anger will find Augustine saying that the Father cannot be angry with humankind, and that it cannot be for anger that the Son died—'Indeed I observe', he continues, citing the same Ephesians passage that she will use, 'that the Father loved us not merely before the Son died for us, but before he founded the world, as the apostle bears witness: *As he chose us in him before the foundation of the world* (Eph. 1: 4)' (XIII. 15). He repeats his argument that evil is privative, not willed by God but merely permitted, giving the same reason that we will find in Julian—that nothing would remain in existence if God did not keep it in being ('How would even the wicked angels go on existing with any sort of life at all but for him *who gives life to everything* (1 Tim. 6: 13)?' (XIII. 16). Augustine, too, says that the trials of this life (Julian's 'irkehede') are the means by which we grow, and that is why they remain when sins have been forgiven (XIII. 20). Augustine is more grimly mordant than Julian—these trials may be useful, he says, for 'demonstrating the wretchedness of this life' so that the next one may be desired more ardently. Nonetheless, his overall conclusion is that all will be well. He draws attention to *imago Dei* and the 'kinship' of Christ as presented by Paul: 'We know that all things work together for good, for those who love God, who are called according to his purpose. For those whom he foreknew he also predestined to be conformed to the image of his Son, in order that he might be the firstborn within a large family' (Rom. 8: 28–9).

God's saving actions are both eternal and, through the Incarnation, temporal. The Johannine prologue leads Augustine to say that eternal truth is rightly attributed to the Word, but 'it is one and the same person by whom deeds were carried out in time for us' (xiii. 24). This means that the subordination of temporal knowledge to eternal wisdom cannot be strictly maintained, for Christ is both.

Christ is *both* our *scientia* and our *sapientia*. The biblical source for this Christian transformation of a pagan distinction, Augustine finds in Col. 2: 3, where Paul says that in Christ 'are hidden all the treasures of wisdom and knowledge'. This passage enables Augustine to provide a condensed summary of his Christology: 'Christ, therefore, is our *scientia* and the same Christ is also our *sapientia*. He himself plants the faith concerning temporal things within us; He Himself manifests the truth concerning eternal things. Through him we travel to Him, through *scientia* we proceed to *sapientia*; but we do not depart from one and the same Christ'[34] The ontological co-ordinates of time and eternity correspond to the epistemological co-ordinates of knowledge and wisdom, all brought together in Christ, who, to continue Augustine's parallelism, is both our homeland and our way. Augustine does not in book XIII return to the gender typology of book XII, but if he had done, he would have been obliged to say that Christ is our Eve as well as our Adam, our rational 'woman' as well as our rational 'man'. The mystery is not that Julian came to see Christ as 'mother', but that Augustine did not.

---

[34] *De Trinitate*, xiii. 24, as cited by Ayres, 'Christological Context', 121. Goulven Madec describes this as a condensed statement of the structure of Augustine's theology: 'Christus, scientia et sapientia nostra: le principe de cohérence de la doctrine augustinienne', *Recherches Augustiniennes*, 10 (1975), 77–85, at 78–9.

Augustine saw clearly that Porphyry's maxim that 'one must completely escape the body' (*omne corpus fugiendun est*) cannot be a Christian one. How does this compare in the end to Julian? Again, it is partly a matter of tone. Augustine accepts that we cannot dismiss our embodied life, while Julian would have us rejoice in it; but both do so by effectively the same means: that is, by finding in Christ, and in Julian's case in the physical body of Christ, our own embodied life's deepest meaning. By mapping our own journey on to his, we find a faith which leads us into a life with God.

As befits works of theology which are spiritual exercises, neither Julian's *Revelation* nor Augustine's *De Trinitate* is presented to us by its author as complete. Nor can they be, for the *imago Dei* is both 'present and yet to be found'.[35] Julian begins her final chapter saying, 'This book is begun by God's gift and his grace, but it is not yet performed, as I see it'—in Middle English, 'not yet performid, as to my syte' (§86). Although he cannot trade on her Middle English association of *travel* and *travail*, the life in Christ is for Augustine, as for Julian, a matter of 'travelling' with God—'Through him we travel to Him (*per ipsum pergimus ad ipsum* )' (XIII. 24). At his book's end he is still praying and seeking:

I have sought you and desired to see intellectually what I have believed, and I have argued much and toiled much. O Lord my God, my one hope, listen to me lest out of weariness I should stop

---

[35] A. N. Williams, 'Contemplation: *Knowledge of God* in Augustine's *de Trinitate*', in D. S. Y. Buckley *et al.* (eds.), *Knowing the Triune God: The Work of the Spirit in the Practices of the Church* (Grand Rapids, Mich.: W. B. Eerdmans, 2001), 121–46, at 137. Williams makes a powerful argument about the dangers of separating, as so much modern writing does, the 'systematic' and the 'mystical' in theology, doctrine from spiritual life (p. 124).

wanting to seek you, but let me seek your face always, and with ardour...Let me remember you, let me understand you, let me love you, Increase these things in me until you refashion me entirely (xv. 51).

It is for the reader to perform the book now.

# 8

# Friendship

BEING called 'the friend of God' may seem tame by comparison with being called God's son or daughter, yet, historically considered, 'friend of God' is amongst the boldest of the biblical epithets. For to have a friend is to be a friend, and if Moses is the friend of God, it follows that God is the friend of Moses—a daring claim. Early Christian theologians were impressed in the highest degree to find that the Lord 'used to speak to Moses face to face, as one speaks to a friend' (Exod. 33: 11). Equally shocking in its way was that Jesus should tell his disciples that they are no longer to be called servants, but friends (John 15: 15). To recapture the strength of this pronouncement, we need to know something of the history of friendship in Western thought.

Christian writings on friendship, right through the Middle Ages, are heavily indebted to Cicero, who is himself already indebted to the Greeks. According to Cicero, the 'one thing in human experience about whose advantage all men with one voice agree, is friendship'. Some men hold virtue in contempt, others disdain riches or political honours, but 'concerning friendship all, to a man, think the same thing... that without friendship life is not life at all'.[1] In the fourth century, Ambrose

[1] Cicero, *Laelius on Friendship*, trans. W. A. Falconer, Loeb Classical Library, 10 (Boston: Harvard University Press, 1923), xxxiii. 86.

157

and Augustine were whole-hearted in their endorsement of Cicero: Augustine thought that Cicero's definition of friendship could not be bettered. Aelred of Rievaulx, writing for twelfth-century monks, finds himself able to cite Cicero almost word for word: 'Friendship is mutual harmony in affairs human and divine coupled with benevolence and charity.'[2]

Indeed, despite some fretful indications that one *should* be able to carve out a distinctly Christian position on friendship— Aelred insists, for instance, that Cicero 'was unacquainted with the virtue of true friendship, since he was completely unaware of its beginning and end, Christ'—Aelred rarely moves far in form or in substance from his pagan master.[3] In this he and other Christian writers were no doubt encouraged by Cicero's own natural theology, notable in the way his definition continues: 'I am inclined to think that with the exception of wisdom no better thing has been given to man by the immortal gods.'[4] Aelred corrects such sentiments only by changing the plural 'gods' to the singular 'God'.[5]

Cicero writes so well and with such warmth that it is not surprising that his sentiments should resound across the ages. Friendship cannot exist except among good men (iv. 18). It contains nothing false or pretended; it arises not from need or desire for material gain, but from love. In friendship two men are equal; indeed, the friend is 'another self', for 'What is

---

[2] Aelred of Rievaulx, *Spiritual Friendship*, trans. Mary E. Laker, SSND (Kalamazoo, Mich.: Cistercian Publications, 1977), book 1, §11 (p. 53). Compare Cicero, *Laelius on Friendship*, vi. 20.

[3] Aelred, *Spiritual Friendship*, book 1, §8 (p. 53).

[4] Cicero, *Laelius on Friendship*, vi. 20.

[5] See, too, Cicero's reproach to those philosophers (probably Stoics) who would say that friendship is a need and a weakness: 'Why, they seem to take the sun out of the universe when they deprive life of friendship, than which we have from the immortal gods no better, no more delightful boon' (ibid. xiii. 47).

sweeter than to have someone with whom you may dare discuss anything *as if you were communing with yourself*?' (vi. 22).

The Greek and Latin literature provides lists of templates, types, and taxonomies of friendship. In the *Nicomachean Ethics* Aristotle gives a threefold classification of friendships, again much used by Christians, based on pleasure, on mutual advantage, and on shared concern for that which is good. All three have their merits, but the third is the best. In Aelred we see what are recognizably the same three more sharply distinguished into carnal, worldly, and spiritual friendships—the first two, in his monastic setting, entirely eclipsed by the third.

We find lists of qualities a friend must have. Cicero would have us seek good men, loyal and upright, fair and generous, free from all passions, caprice, and insolence, with great strength of character (v. 19), frank, sociable, sympathetic (xviii. 65), candid, affable, genial, agreeable, wholly courteous, and urbane (xvii. 66). This list of desiderata surely must limit the number of likely candidates to be anyone's friend.

In our own time friendship is more frequently discussed by social scientists than by philosophers or theologians. Sociologists, psychologists, and anthropologists study 'friendship' as a 'natural' phenomenon—biologically adaptive and functionally effective—not Cicero's approach at all. Theologians spill more ink on 'love', and understandably so, since some of the most stirring sayings of the New Testament concern love—'love your enemies', 'God is love'. If God is love, then why look further for affective relationships? Love is, indeed, all you need. By comparison, friendship is love's pale echo.

Notoriously, some Christian theologians have tried to rank the Greek notion of *agapē* and that of *philia*, privileging *agapē* as the truly Christian form of love—a love which knows no bounds and loves without cause or concern. We need to be cautious about such rankings. In classical writings, 'love' and 'friendship' flow into one another. Cicero several times makes the point that for him it is more than etymological—*amicitia* (friendship) derives from *amor*, and in the Greek of the New Testament *agapē* and *philia* overlap in use.[6] In any case, it seems fundamentally mistaken to suppose that we can honour love only by disparaging friendship. The latter is not so much love's competitor as a particular manifestation of it. Friendship is best considered not in contrast to love's gold standard, but rather as what friendship 'is', distinct and in itself.

Friendships are particular and partial. You are friends with particular people and not with everyone, and this gives friendship a different scope from love even within the Christian lexicon. You should, according to the Scriptures, love your neighbour and even your enemy. You cannot be *friends* with everybody without evacuating 'friendship' of all meaning. Cicero marks this as a difference between friendship and relationship (*propinquitas*): good will can be removed from a relationship but not from friendship, since 'if you remove goodwill from friendship the very name of friendship is gone' (v. 19).

Friendship is reciprocal—it involves at least two. A lover may have a beloved, but we can readily think of circumstances where love is not returned. Love can be unrequited or love for an admired figure from the past. Although we may doubt whether we can *love* our enemies (*not* a sentiment to be found

<hr />

[6] One thinks here especially of Anders Nygren, but also of Kierkegaard. On this and for many other insights, see Gillian Clark and Stephen R. L. Clark, 'Friendship in the Christian Tradition', in R. Porter and S. Tomaselli (eds.), *The Dialectics of Friendship* (London and New York: Routledge, 1989), 26–43.

in Cicero), the New Testament enjoins us to do so, with no suggestion that they will love us back. We also read that it was not we who first loved God, but God who first loved us. So love, like hatred, need not be reciprocal or symmetrical: I can love without being loved, have an enemy without being one.

I can love without being loved, but friendship is quite different. I might say I love Nelson Mandela, whom I have never met, but I cannot say that he is one of my friends. I cannot say, except in a deliberately contentious sense, 'I am *his* friend but he is not mine.' To be a friend is to have a friend.

If love is divine, then friendship is, in its fundamental aspect, human. Friendship demands a certain distance as well as an intimacy between the one and the other. Christians can and do speak of the love flowing between the three Persons of the Trinity, but it would be unwise, in Trinitarian terms, to say that the three 'Persons' are friends of each other: that would be a sentiment dangerously near to tritheism, although we might be able to say 'the Trinity is friendship' much as one says 'God is love'.[7]

Friendship, I suggest, is fundamentally a creaturely and, more specifically, a human good. There are of course many 'goods for us' which cannot be predicated of God. It is good for us to eat, laugh, swim, and play musical instruments. It is good for us to breathe, walk, and have red blood cells. All these are creaturely goods and, the Christian doctrine of the Incarnation apart, good for God only in so far as we are God's creatures and what is 'good' for his creatures is, in a sense, 'good' for God.

---

[7] When Ivo, in the dialogue, asks Aelred, 'Shall I say of friendship what John, the friend of Jesus, says of charity: "God is friendship"?' (cf. 1 John 4: 16), Aelred replies that while this is unusual and does not have the sanction of Scripture, 'what is true of charity I surely do not hesitate to grant to friendship' (*Spiritual Friendship*, Book 1, §§ 69–70 (pp. 65–6).

Not all creatures have the same goods. It is good for a bird to have feathers, but not for a snake; good for a rabbit to have warm, furry ears, but not for a fish. We need, then, some anthropology, some concept of the human being, to understand friendship as a distinctly human good. Here I confess myself to be suspicious of those anthropologies that undergird aspirational theories of friendship like that of Cicero—friendships springing from nature rather than from need. I have my doubts concerning this winnowing of men in a search for the truly virtuous, for the flash of soul upon soul. I hesitate over this search for men loyal and upright, fair and generous, free from all passions, caprice, and insolence, frank, sociable, sympathetic, candid, affable, genial, agreeable, wholly courteous, and urbane (xvii. 66). Aelred at least makes our task a little easier, in a departure from Cicero, by listing not *what to seek* in a friend but *what to avoid*. We should avoid the irascible, the fickle, the suspicious, the garrulous, the angry, the unstable, the avaricious, and the ambitious.[8] Now all this is good advice and, let us hope, advice that could be pursued in a twelfth-century Cistercian cloister; but we may ask, this side of eternity, where could one find such a friend? Even more daunting, how could one be such a friend? Do these directives not presuppose superhuman self-knowledge, as well as a preternatural insight as to the inner workings of our neighbour? I want an anthropology at once more earthly than Cicero's and, at the same time, more genuinely divine.

In 1960 C. S. Lewis published a popular and influential little book entitled *The Four Loves*. Friendship is one of these four, and Lewis, improbably, anchors it in the relations of the primal

---

[8] Ibid. book 3, §14 (p. 94), *passim*.

horde. Speaking throughout of 'male friendship'—since, he tells us, friendship will in most societies and periods be between men and men or women and women—he provides a little creative ethnography: 'In early communities the co-operation of the males as hunters or fighters was no less necessary than the begetting and rearing of children... Long before history began we men have got together apart from the women and done things. We had to.' He continues with a jovial pun, 'Palaeolithic man may or may not have had a club on his shoulder but he certainly had a club of the other sort, a sort of "early sacred smoking-club".'[9]

From this basic 'clubbableness', as Lewis terms it, friendship arises on the basis of shared insight, interest, and vision. Modern friends 'will still be doing something together, but something more inward... still hunters, but of some immaterial quarry'.[10] This, he tells us, is 'the luminous, tranquil, rational world of relationships freely chosen'. Friendship on his account is the least organic of loves, and thus differentiated from the tugging of the guts and the fluttering of the diaphragm that characterize *Affection*, which we have for our young, and *Eros*, which we have for the opposite sex.[11] Women are to all intents and purposes ruled out of this happy band. Friendships between the sexes easily and quickly pass into erotic love (even within the first half

---

[9] C. S. Lewis, *The Four Loves* (1960) (London: Fount, 1998), 60. He continues: 'What were women doing meanwhile? How should I know? I am a man. I can trace the pre-history of friendship only in the male line' (p. 61). He does not explain how he knows what *men* were doing in prehistoric times.

[10] Ibid. 62. It will be apparent that this is Lewis at his most insufferably 'donnish'.

[11] Ibid. 56. Lewis goes out of his way to distance this real manly friendship from homosexuality: 'Hrothgar embracing Beowulf, Johnson embracing Boswell (a pretty flagrantly heterosexual couple)' (ibid. 59).

hour, according to Lewis) unless, of course, the two are lucky enough to be physically repulsive to one another. Thus, he says, 'it will be clear that in most societies at most periods Friendship will be between men and men or women and women. The sexes will have met one another in Affection and in Eros but not in this love.'[12] Even with his own wife or lover, then, a man will share Affection and Eros but not friendship.

Lewis's manly friendship is highly streamlined: 'You become a man's Friend without knowing or caring whether he is married or single or how he earns is living. What have all these "unconcerning things, matters of fact" to do with the real question, *Do you see the same truth?*. No one cares two-pence about anyone else's family, profession, class, income, race or previous history.' This love (essentially) ignores not only our physical bodies but that whole embodiment which consists of our family, job, past, and connections. Whereas Eros will have naked bodies, friendship is 'an affair of disentangled, or stripped minds'.[13]

Lewis's account of friendship is recognizably Ciceronian, but without Cicero's human warmth. Cicero is at least willing to speak of friendships, not albeit of the highest kind, between children and their parents, or between a man and the nurses and slaves who tended him when a child, and even between animals and their young. Lewis takes to an extreme the Ciceronian ideal of a friend as *alter ego*. And it is important to see that what is unsatisfactory about friendships with women on this account is not their sexual allure, something

<hr />

[12] Ibid. 68.    [13] Ibid. 66–7.

which troubled Ambrose and Augustine when it came to the question of friendships with women, but the fact that women will not share the same interests and activities as men—they are not like 'us', for 'they [men and women] will seldom have had with each other the companionship in common activities which is the matrix of friendship'.[14] What of the emotional world of these 'stripped minds'? How, we wonder, would Lewis react if another 'stripped mind' arrived at the club and told him that his child had been knocked off a bicycle and was mortally ill? Blustering silence?—'terribly sorry, old boy, didn't know you were married—had offspring—that sort of thing... but let's get on with translating Beowulf'. How can we love someone or be friends with someone in their distinct particularity without knowing what they love? Stripped of all distinctiveness, the other is an *alter ego* only in a parodic sense—a mirror in which I see myself reflected.[15] It is not the exclusivity of this vision which should concern us, for friendship must always be particular, but rather that it rules out as a possibility friendship with one who is distinctively other. No doubt Lewis's practice was better than his theory, but there is something sterile and self-regarding about Lewis's sketch of friendship here, something which took a terrific blow when he fell in love with an other who was an American, a Jew, and a divorcee.[16]

It is not surprising that, despite being the most 'spiritual' of the four loves in his reckoning (that is, the least biological), friendship has, for Lewis, little directly to do with God. He does

[14] Ibid. 68.
[15] Lewis's sketch, while not homosexual, is certainly 'hommosexual' in Luce Irigaray's sense—a panegyric of love between same and same.
[16] Lewis writes of this movingly in *A Grief Observed*, originally published under a pseudonym in 1961.

not want to speak of God as a friend. Surprisingly, for a writer so committed to the Bible, he does not mention any of the biblical passages which speak of friendship with God. On the contrary, it is better, he says, to speak of God as father or as husband, language that cannot be taken literally. Nor *can* Lewis speak of God as 'friend', since a friend is for him, by definition, another self, an *alter ego*, and God must be further away, holier, than that. There is no room for friendship with the genuinely other, and therefore certainly not for friendship with God.

This distortion may allow us to see, amongst the gold, some iron pyrite in Cicero's famous account of friendship, which is, after all, not in the least egalitarian. It goes without saying that for Cicero the highest form of friendship is found only between males, men who are virtuous and wise, share common goals and aspirations, and rich enough so as not to need the friend-ship in any material way.[17] The *alter ego* is an image of the good man's virtuous self.

Aelred's Christian version is more attractive. His is not a picture of a perfect male society, although to some extent he inhabited one. There are no women in his circle, but he does speak of the creation of Eve from the very stuff of Adam and as his equal, and of the primal pair as a most beautiful inspiration as to what charity and friendship might be. Nonetheless, Aelred's account of spiritual friendship retains some of the static features that limit Cicero's. What, were it ever achieved, would friendship have been like between monastic paragons? Would it be like the friendships of angels or of celestial spheres, whose movements were so perfect they neither needed to be, nor could

---

[17] In our time this is why it is not enough to put too much weight on the power of 'discussion' if we have not first considered who is, and is not, in fact present as a discussion partner—who is present at friendship's table?

be, tuned? And is it not the case that, in this world, we bump along—fragile, forgetful, and all too human in our failings?

Let us approach this from a different starting point, not Cicero but the Book of Exodus:

Now Moses used to take the tent and pitch it outside the camp, far off from the camp; he called it the tent of meeting. And everyone who sought the LORD would go out to the tent of meeting... Whenever Moses went out to the tent, all the people would rise... the pillar of cloud would descend and stand at the entrance of the tent, and the LORD would speak with Moses... the LORD used to speak to Moses face to face, as one speaks to a friend (Exod. 33: 7–11a).

The Lord would speak with Moses face to face, *as a man speaks with his friend.*

Friendship, I have argued, is not an affective bond which may or may not be requited. It is not, as Aristotle knew, a 'virtue' from which some other may or may not benefit, but a *relationship*. In this relationship, 'the other person enters in not just as an object who receives the good activity, but as an intrinsic part of the love itself.'[18] An anthropology adequate to friendship would be an anthropology of the-at-least-two, the one and the other who may reach out to include a third and a fourth. I suggest that we might look for such an anthropology to the writings of Martin Buber and of his friend and associate Franz Rosenzweig—to Buber's 'dialogical principle' and to Rosenzweig's philosophy of 'speaking thinking'. For both Buber and Rosenzweig the human being was essentially a 'speaking' being.

While ample and perplexed consideration has been given to the question of how it is that God may speak to us (for instance, in revelation), far less has been paid to the fact,

---

[18] A. J. P. Kenny, *Aristotle on the Perfect Life* (Oxford: Clarendon Press, 1992), 43.

equally mysterious and wonderful, that we speak to each other. We take our capacity for speech for granted, but no other animal speaks one to another in the elaborate, diffuse, and unpredictable way we do. No other animal makes a promise or, in the truest sense, tells a lie.

Let me recall that passage of his *Speeches on Religion* where Schleiermacher pauses to reflect on Adam alone in Eden.[19] As long as Adam was alone, he says, God addressed him in various ways; but Adam did not understand, for he did not answer. Adam's paradise was beautiful, but he could not fully sense it. He did not 'even develop within his soul'. Naming the animals brought no solace to Adam, but only greater dereliction. It was not until there was another human being that his silence was broken and Adam could, for the first time, see the glory of what lay about him and praise its Creator.[20] Schleiermacher turns this mythical reverie into an anthropological observation whose truth is empirical as much as metaphysical. Without other persons, one would not speak. This is true of any individual—no infant, apart from being taught to speak by other people, would do so. It is also true of the human race in general: were there only one man, there could not be language—this is Wittgenstein's point in the private language argument. Language is a social possession and a social phenomenon. Without others we would not have language, and without language we would not be ourselves. Even those human beings not yet fully in the realm of language (for example, newborns) and those

[19] I discuss this at greater length in J. M. Soskice, 'Incarnation, Speech and Sociality in Schleiermacher and Augustine', in M. M. Olivetti (ed.), *Incarnation*, Proceedings of the Castelli Colloquium (Padua: cedam, 1999).

[20] Schleiermacher, *On Religion: Speeches to its Cultured Despisers*, ed. Crouter; *idem, On Religion*, ed. R. Crouter (Cambridge: Cambridge University Press, 1988), 119.

who may never fully acquire language are spoken to, spoken of, and cared for by speaking beings whose shared power of speech enables them to do all they do. We are brought into life by those others who bring us into language as much as by those who bear us physically in their wombs. Even our private thoughts are framed and formed in the language we share with others.[21]

A sustained meditation on the sociality of speaking is to be found in Martin Buber's philosophy of 'dialogue', presented in 1923 in *I and Thou*[22] and developed in other essays. It is a mistake to read Buber as an existentialist, as I was directed to do when I first read him, if we mean by that a solitary, fraught soul in search of meaning. Indeed, Buber rejects any quest for human identity that begins with the solitary self or, indeed, with the collective 'mankind'. The essence of man is found neither in the individual nor in the collectivity, but only in the reality of mutual relations 'between man and man'.[23]

What Buber called his 'turn to the other' accompanied a dramatic change in his understanding of 'the religious'. In the essay 'Dialogue', written in 1929 to clarify the dialogical principle of *I and Thou*, he writes—somewhat elliptically—about this:

---

[21] This is not the same as saying that our thought is predetermined by language. It is interesting to note that Aelred and Cicero have similar thought experiments to Schleiermacher's. Aelred asks his young monastic if, had he all the possessions, riches, and delights in the world—'gold, silver, precious stones, turreted camps, spacious buildings, sculptures, and paintings'—but no companion, would he enjoy all these possessions. Walter answers 'not at all'. Aelred then says, 'But suppose there were one person, whose language you did not know, of whose customs you were ignorant, whose love and heart lay concealed from you?' Walter says, 'If I could not by some signs make him a friend, I should prefer to have no one at all rather than to have such a one' (*Spiritual Friendship*, book 3, §78 (p. 110)).

[22] M. Buber, *I and Thou: With a Postscript by the Author Added* (Edinburgh: T. & T. Clark, 1958).

[23] Martin Buber, Foreword to M. Buber, *Between Man and Man*, trans. Ronald G. Smith (London: Kegan Paul, 1947), p. vii.

In my earlier years the 'religious' was for me the exception. There were hours that were taken out of the course of things. From somewhere or other the firm crust of everyday was pierced ... 'Religious experience' was the experience of an otherness which did not fit into the context of life.[24]

One forenoon, 'after a morning of "religious" enthusiasm, I had a visit from a young man ...'. Buber's account of this meeting is sketchy, but while being friendly and even listening attentively, Buber felt that he had failed to hear this young person. He failed to discern in him an anguish about which he found out only after the young man was dead, it is implied by his own hand:

Since then I have given up the 'religious' which is nothing but the exception, extraction, exaltation, ecstasy; or it has given me up. I possess nothing now but the everyday out of which I am never taken ... I know no fullness but each moral hour's fullness of claim and responsibility. Though far from being equal to it, yet I know that in the claim I am claimed and may respond in responsibility, and know who speaks and demands a response.

Here we have the this–here–now of existentialism, but always tied by Buber to the presence of the other: 'I do not know much more. If that is religion then it is just *everything*, simply all that is lived in its possibility of dialogue.'[25] This is more than a speaking *at* one another. It is more than just exchanging pleasantries or pieces of information: 'the most eager speaking at one another does not make a conversation (this is most clearly shown in that curious sport, aptly termed discussion, that is

---

[24] Martin Buber, Foreword to M. Buber, *Between Man and Man*, trans. Ronald G. Smith (London: Kegan Paul, 1947), 13.
[25] Ibid. 13–14.

"breaking apart", which is indulged in by men who are to some extent gifted with the ability to think).'[26] It has equally little to do with those fictitious conversations which pass for religious dialogues 'where none regarded and addressed his partner in reality'.[27] As a meeting of the open-hearted with the open-hearted, dialogue can even be found expressive in appropriate moments of silence. Those who have been consoled by a good friend in grief or in sorrow will know the moment.

Monologue, or rather monologue disguised as dialogue, is treated by Buber with contempt. If the basic life of dialogue is a turning towards the other, then the basic life of the monologist is not a turning away from, for to turn away, one needs already at least to have *noticed* the other, but rather a 'reflexion', where the other is not met as an other at all, but merely as an aspect on the monological self. An example Buber gives is the lover's chat, which, far from being an ideal of intimacy, is little more than a dual monologue 'in which both partners alike enjoy their own glorious soul and their precious experience.'[28] (This is rather like that of Mme de Stael—'égoisme à deux'.) Just as the verbose do not necessarily speak, the monologist is not necessarily a solitary. He may be in the midst of the social swim, a politician, a preacher, a campaigner for good causes, but never stop to speak 'from being to being' with a fellow man.[29] In a parallel way (and here Buber anticipates elements of environmental philosophy), the natural world is treated either as a glorious state of the soul (an *état d'âme*) or as a passive object of knowledge, either completely internalized in the life of feeling or completely externalized to the

---

[26] Ibid. 3.
[27] Ibid. 8. Buber, writing in 1929, seemed to anticipate a new dawn of conversations between the faiths—a tragic hope when we reflect that the Shoah followed.
[28] Ibid. 20.    [29] Ibid.

world 'out there'.[30] The one living the life of monologue, above all, 'is never aware of the other as something that is *absolutely not himself* and at the same time something with which he nevertheless communicates'.[31] Whereas 'Being, lived in dialogue, receives even in extreme dereliction a harsh and strengthening sense of reciprocity; being, lived in monologue, will not, even in the tenderest intimacy, grope out over the outlines of the self.'[32]

Religion is the most deceptive retreat for the monologist, especially when this represents an attempt to find union with the One by casting off the dross of 'mere humanity'. 'This person is not nearer but more distant from the God who is turned to men and who gives himself as the *I* to a *Thou* and the *Thou* to an *I*.'[33]

It is important to see that, despite his expressionist rhetoric, Buber is not calling for a 'universal unreserve' that requires intimacy with every one we meet, and indeed, that he has put a serious question mark beside some interpretations of the Christian 'Love your neighbour'.[34] He *is* saying that one must be ready to stand in relation to others, and even to meet and be changed by others who are not one's *alter ego*/own type, but rather, 'absolutely not' oneself. Buber's is, in the end, a disciplined and austere religious vision. In it one seeks not perfection, but just a 'breakthrough' into 'nothing exalted, heroic or holy, into no Either or no Or'. He describes this in a beautiful phrase as the 'tiny strictness and grace of the everyday'.[35]

---

[30] Martin Buber, Foreword to M. Buber, *Between Man and Man*, trans. Ronald G. Smith (London: Kegan Paul, 1947), 19, 20.

[31] Ibid. 20, my emphasis.　　　[32] Ibid.　　　[33] Ibid. 25.

[34] Buber's style does not please all readers, yet one can see why, in an effort to burst through the starched formality of the philosophical writings of his day, his writing verges on the vatic.

[35] Ibid. 36.

In what is one of the most theologically revealing moments in his 'Dialogue' Buber says, 'Only when two say to one another with all that they are, "It is *Thou*", is the indwelling of the Present Being between them.' The 'indwelling of the Present Being' here is the Shekinah, 'the place where the Lord God causes his name to dwell.'[36]

*I and Thou* is the fruit of reflections that absorbed Buber between 1918 and 1923, influenced by his reading of Hermann Cohen and his conversations with Franz Rosenzweig. By 1919 Buber had written a draft of the book and was already describing Jewish teaching as 'two-directional, as a reciprocal relation existing between the human I and the divine Thou'.[37] The deeply Jewish nature of the book was to some extent concealed from its first audience, partly by Buber himself, who wished to give the book a broader appeal, and partly by a readership little attuned to his religious message.[38] *I and Thou* came late as a title. Buber had earlier referred to it as the 'Prolegomena to a Philosophy of Religion' or, more tellingly, 'Religion as Presence'.[39] In 1922, and thus a year before the publication of *I and Thou*, he gave a course entitled 'Religion as Presence' (*Religion als Gegenwart*) at a Jewish college.[40] Evident in these lectures, though downplayed in

[36] Ibid. 30. Cf. Deut. 12: 11 (see the Translator's note on p. 207).

[37] Ibid. 20.

[38] Rivka Horwitz says that those whose orientation was to social philosophy read *I and Thou* as social philosophy, and judged its references to God and religion to be inessential. The truth, according to Horowitz, is the other way around: the social aspects were added to a work 'whose original and primary concern was the attempt, prompted by the disillusion with mysticism, to reformulate the concept and position of religion' R. Horwitz and M. Buber, *Buber's Way to 'I and Thou': An Historical Analysis and the First Publication of Martin Buber's Lectures 'Religion als Gegenwart'* (Heidelberg: Schneider, 1978), 29.

[39] Ibid. 22.

[40] These lectures were published for the first time only in 1978 by Rivka Horwitz, in the book cited in n. 39 above.

the published *I and Thou*, is the fact that the template for the meeting of man with man is the meeting of Moses with God on Sinai. This is the *God who is present* to Israel, the God who addresses Moses from the burning bush, and who is, in turn addressed by him. For Buber, as for Rosenzweig, this moment is of decisive importance. When translating the Bible the two pondered at length over the proper translation of the Hebrew 'name' given to Moses in Exod. 3: 14, the name frequently rendered in English language Bibles as 'I AM WHO I AM'. In their opinion— and scholarly opinion both Jewish and Christian is with them on this—'I AM WHO I AM' is not, in Exodus, a metaphysical utterance. Here is a gloss of Rosenzweig's, expressing a translator's viewpoint that the two shared,

> ...all those who find here notions of 'being,' of 'the-one-who-is,' of 'the eternal,' are all Platonizing...God calls himself not 'the-one-who-is' but 'the one-who-is-there,' i.e. there for you, there for you at this place, present to you, with you or rather coming toward you, toward you to help you. For the Hebrew *hayah* is not, unlike the Indo-Germanic 'to be,' of its nature a copula, not of its nature static, but a word of becoming, of entering, of happening.[41]

This relationship with the Absolute Thou stands, for Buber, behind all our being present to others: the German *Gegenwart* indicates both 'presence' and 'present'. The Absolute Thou is the presence which guarantees that religion cannot be past—only present. In the lectures, though not in the book, Buber is pleased to identify this presence with the Shekinah.

---

[41] 'A Letter to Martin Goldner', in M. Buber and F. Rosenzweig, *Scripture and Translation*, trans. Lawrence Rosenwald with Everett Fox (Bloomington: Indiana University Press, 1994), 191.

# Friendship

The same themes run through Rosenzweig's philosophy of 'speaking thinking'. This is thinking always done in genuine response to another and allowing of difference. It is modest, in allowing that the other may have something to tell us, yet not fearful. In contrast to the Hegelian pattern, where thesis and antithesis sublate one another to be mutually annihilated in synthesis, in dialogical thinking the one and the other one are not destroyed by their encounter, but become more truly themselves. In contrast to philosophy's claim to speak from a timeless nowhere, actual speech is 'bound by time and nourished by time'. Because of this, dialogue 'does not know in advance just where it will end. It takes its cue from others.' Unlike the *faux* dialogues of Plato or Hume, where the philosopher controls and brings the dialogue to a predetermined destiny, 'In actual conversation, something happens.' We are changed. 'Perhaps the other person will say the first word for in a true conversation this is usually the case; a glance at the Gospels and the Socratic dialogues will show the contrast.'[42]

These two Jewish writers, Buber and Rosenzweig, can provide the foundations for an anthropology of the-at-least-two, remedial to Christian, or Western, tendencies to privilege the solitary self. We are told that young people take friendship more seriously than they do marriage, but what kind of friendship? Is the ideal put before us that of a friendship that does not

---

[42] 'The New Thinking: Philosophy and Religion', in F. Rosenzweig, *Franz Rosenzweig: His Life and Thought*, trans. N. N. Glatzer (Indianapolis and Cambridge: Hackett, 1998), 198–9. I am warmed by Rosenzweig's suggestion that the Gospels, and he must mean their accounts of Jesus, show someone who is a 'speaking thinker', someone who is actually hearing and responding. Christianity has not proved so good at this.

disturb us too much? A friend can be a friend as long as he or she does not make too many demands? While the 'self as solitary cogito' characteristic of much early modern and Enlightenment philosophical writing has been subjected to damning philosophical criticism, what might be called the 'popular' modern self (that is, the notion of self, placed, flattered, and cajoled by the advertising industry, the media, self-help gurus, and even some philosophy) is still fundamentally autarchic after the eighteenth-century pattern and pictures of the self as (ideally) fully self-ruling and self-possessed, dipping into association with others as this suits a private end. Cicero would more likely call this *propinquitas* than *amicitia*.

But within an anthropology of the-at-least-two, the friend is not a blank sheet for the free play of my emotions or a mirror for my virtues. Nor are the friends aligned in Cicero's symmetrical and essentially static perfection; rather, I am becoming myself in and through who I am for others and who they are for me. Friendship is in this sense an eschatological relationship, for it has as much to do with what I may become as with what I now am.

Who can be my friend? Not *everyone*, and certainly not everyone at once. Friendship is a relation with particular persons and not with generic humanity. But if we cannot be friends with everyone, we should not dismiss the un-Ciceronian possibility that we might be friends with *anyone*. Buber prompts us to consider the possibility that a friend may come—as a surprise—a grace. Friends cannot after all be mechanically generated. Like the divine 'You', there is a sense in which the human you encounters me by grace—it cannot be found by seeking. And because friendship is not based on shared perfection in virtue, and is not static, within this way of thinking there is room to say that we might become the friends of God.

*Friendship*

We become who we are, and know who we are to the limited extent in which we genuinely 'know ourselves', through our relationships with other people. Because our speaking to one another in true conversation is never complete, we can never know ourselves to be completed, finished products.

# CONCLUSION

> From the very beginning every thought of Dostoevsky's heroes (the 'underground man', Raskolnikov, Ivan, etc.) feels itself to be a *speech* in an uncompleted dialog. Such a thought does not pursue a rounded-off and finalized monological whole. It lives a tense life on the border of another idea and another consciousness.
>
> Mikhail Bakhtin

We might ask what it is for us today to write philosophy in a way mindful of 'the-at-least-two'? Can the *writing* of philosophy be separated from what it is to *read* philosophy? And what is it to write philosophy when one's subject is 'reverence for the other', or even intersubjectivity? The philosophical writer has a dilemma; to write a piece of philosophy is in most cases to write a monologue. It is to write a work in which the author, in prescriptive mode, lays down definitions, imposes structure, and provides analysis. As a monologue, the text of philosophy has no capacity and no textual place to *listen* to another. Even texts of philosophy that are putative dialogues, like Hume's *Dialogues Concerning Natural Religion*, are, on closer observation, tightly controlled by their authors. This may be more than a problem of style, for an anthropology of the-at-least-two is at odds with the

autarchic subject cultivated by so much modern philosophy—
self-contained and self-ruling, for whom the rupture towards the
other could come only as a wound.

To challenge this modernist conception of individual autonomy was the aspiration of a truly great twentieth-century theorist
of dialogue, Mikhail Bakhtin. Hailed in the West by Left-leaning
intellectuals in the 1960s as a Marxist standard-bearer, Bakhtin
now emerges, subsequent to the opening of Soviet archives in the
early 1990s, as one whose 'first and most obvious context is not
Marxism but Orthodoxy',[43] perhaps even a *staretz* or saint. The
attentive reader can see the clues in works like *Problems in
Dostoevsky's Poetics*. Dostoevsky's genius, according to Bakhtin,
is to break with the monological tradition of the novel in which
the author controls the plot, the characters, the sentiments of the
hero who is an object of the author's word.[44] It was the genius of
Dostoevsky to create an entirely new form in which the author
creates not 'voiceless slaves (as does Zeus), but rather *free* people
who are capable of standing beside their creator, of disagreeing
with him, and even of rebelling against him'. Responding sharply
to an anti-Semitic remark by one of his disciples, Bakhtin said,
'The Jews have argued with God, made peace with Him, accepted
and rejected his Grace ... And we Russians, what have we done?
Thrown Perun into the river?'[45]

This is Bakhtin's 'polyphonic' novel, and its antecedents are as
much in biblical narratives as in Marxist dialectics. When Bakhtin
praises Dostoevsky for affirming 'the next man's "I" not as an

---

[43] C. Lock, 'Reviewing Bakhtin', *St Vladimir's Theological Quarterly*, 43/1
(1999), 86. See also A. Mihailovic, *Corporeal Words: Mikhail Bakhtin's Theology
of Discourse* (Evanston, Ill.: Northwestern University Press, 1997), Introduction.

[44] M. M. Bakhtin, *Problems of Dostoevsky's Poetics*, trans. R. W. Rotsel (Ann
Arbor: Ardis, 1973), 3.

[45] Ibid. 14–15. Perun was a Slavic pagan deity.

object but as another subject', and adds that 'The heroes must affirm another man's "Thou art" in order to overcome their ethical solipsism', it is difficult not to hear echoes of Buber.[46] Certainly Bakhtin has read and been influenced by both Husserl, on intersubjectivity, and Hermann Cohen, whose writings inspired the dialogical theories of both Buber and Rosenzweig. Bakhtin tells us clearly that his vision is not *dialectical*: 'if the ideas in the novel were arranged as links in a unified dialectical series, then each novel would be a complete philosophical whole—the final link in the dialectical series would be the author's synthesis, cancelling out the previous ones as superceded.'[47]

The important thing is not a dialectical unfolding within a monological conception, but rather 'the important thing is the final dialogicality' of the whole, and the template for this would seem to be the Bible, whose heroes are never objects but always subjects, predestined to be free (and argumentative) by the divine author. Bakhtin's own theory of dialogue is also a meditation on the Word made flesh, the Word becoming real when people speak to one another.[48]

How might this dialogical polyphony work in texts of philosophy of religion? Patristic and medieval theology make use of epistolary genres, the contrapuntal style of medieval *Quaestiones Disputatae*, and prayer. Perhaps the text most redolent with what Bakhtin admires in Dostoevsky is Augustine's philosophical prose-prayer, the *Confessions*, which, despite appearances, is not a

---

[46] Bahktin, *Problems of Dostoevsky's Poetics*, 7. Bakhtin is citing another critic, Ivanov, with approval. I am told by Paul Mendes-Flohr that Bakhtin was a reader of Buber, although neither he nor I can find now the source for this.

[47] Ibid. 21.

[48] This essentially Johannine theme runs behind his theory of discourse *(slovo)*, for in Russian *slovo* is the term used to translate *logos* in the Fourth Gospel. See Mihailovic, *Corporeal Words*, ch. 1, for an extensive treatment of this theme.

monologue. Augustine's silent interlocutor is God. Nor is Augustine's the only human voice in the text: by constant immersion in the words of Scripture, Augustine invokes his teachers in faith—the psalmists, prophets, and disciples—whose voices stream across the pages to a new audience of the faithful who are Augustine's addressees. His 'introspection' leads to no autarchic self and no clear-lit chamber of subjectivity, but to the acknowledgement that we remain mysteries to ourselves, known by God. Because the work is a work of praise (*confessio*), it can never be completed or will be complete only in the *City of God*. In the meantime, we must all live, attentively and like Dostoevsky's characters, on the 'tense life on the border of another idea and another consciousness'. In speaking and listening to one another, we grow and change. This is friendship.

# 9

# Being Lovely: Eschatological Anthropology

LITERALLY, eschatology concerns 'the last things': death, resurrection, the new creation, but also the future hope of the individual, of the *ecclesia*, and of the created order. Anthropology in the Bible is never wholly separate from eschatology, nor creation from redemption, because 'what we will be' is not separable from what we were made to be and what we now are. We should perhaps speak, in the New Testament, of an *eschatological anthropology* in which we are loved, we will love, and we will be made lovely in our Lord Jesus Christ.

Kinship imagery is well suited to the 'already now and not yet' of Christian hope, because the child, wife, or brother has an established and certain relationship with a mother, a husband, or sister—but one with room for growth. So too the Christian life is one in which the believer is 'born again', not into static perfection, but into a new life which must be characterized by growth and transformation.

From their first appearances in the Old Testament, kinship metaphors contain the mixture of promise and challenge proper to an eschatological anthropology. Thus in the Song of Moses in Deuteronomy God chastises the people Israel: is not God your father who created you? Have you forgotten the Rock which gave your birth? (Deut. 32: 1–18), and Jeremiah even speaks of God's longing for the time when Israel will be both child and spouse: 'And I thought you would call me, My Father, and would not turn from following me. Instead, as a faithless wife leaves her husband, so you have been faithless to me, O house of Israel' (Jer. 3: 196–20). Already in the Old Testament God is portrayed as thirsting for ever greater at-one-ment with the created order, and especially humankind. In the New Testament St Paul especially sees this longed-for filiation as achieved through the ministry of the Son:

he chose us in Christ before the foundation of the world to be holy and blameless before him in love. He destined us for adoption as his children through Jesus Christ, according to the good pleasure of his will, to the praise of his glorious grace that he freely bestowed on us in the Beloved (Eph. 1: 4–6).

But it would be wrong to think that whereas the Old Testament prophets long for the consummation of divine longing, the New Testament sees it as finally complete. St Paul portrays the faithful, and indeed the whole created order, as sighing for the final, promised deliverance: 'We know that the whole creation has been groaning in labour pains until now; and not only the creation, but we ourselves, who have the first fruits of the Spirit, groan inwardly while we wait for adoption, the redemption of our bodies' (Rom. 8: 22–3).[1] This 'now and not-yet-ness', so familiar in Paul's writings, should warn us away from presumption about the 'last things', particularly if this presumption constrains the grace, the kindness, of God.

---

[1] Paul goes on immediately to speak of Christ as the 'firstborn' of a large family.

We do not here see clearly, but as in a mirror. We know that we are loved by God, but cannot imagine the fullness of that love, or who and what it will embrace.

In a sermon on the Song of Songs Bernard of Clairvaux raises the question of why, if God is unchanging, he appears to us in so many ways? Bernard saw Christ in all the figures of the Song of Songs—the bashful bridegroom, the physician with oils and ointments, the travelling companion. In the New Testament, too, after the death of Christ, the disciples see, but do not always recognize, their risen Lord. When Mary Magdalene first saw the risen Christ, she thought he was a gardener, and the disciples on the road to Emmaus did not know him until he broke bread with them. Bernard explains that the deficiency is not God's, but ours: for the present the Lord does not 'appear to all in a similar manner, but as the Apostle says: "in many and various ways," still remaining one in himself, in accord with his word to Israel: "The Lord your God is one God."'[2] And the reason why we, and even the disciples, do not yet see him as he truly is, is because we are not yet what we are destined to become: 'Beloved, we are God's children now; what we will be has not yet been revealed. What we do know is this: when he is revealed, we will be like him, for we will see him as he is' (1 John 3: 2). Bernard has noticed the marvellous double hiddenness in this verse: we do not yet know fully what we will be, because we do not yet know fully the glory of God. For now we have only glimpses.

Contemplating the soul, progressing on its itinerary of love and poised between this world and the next, St Bonaventure says that

---

[2] Bernard of Clairvaux, Sermon 31, in *On the Song of Songs*, ii, trans. Kilian J. Walsh (Kalamazoo, Mich.: Cistercian Publications, 1983), 127. Bernard is citing Heb. 1: 1; Deut. 6: 4.

Filled with all these intellectual illuminations,
our mind, like the house of God
is inhabited by divine Wisdom;
it is made
a daughter of God, his spouse and friend;
it is made
a member of Christ the Head, his sister and coheir;
it is made
a temple of the Holy Spirit,
grounded on faith, built up by hope
and dedicated to God.[3]

Bonaventure's biblically sculpted vision of human perfection is here in feminine mode by medieval custom, and because he has in mind the vision of the heavenly Jerusalem of the Book of Revelation (Rev. 21). Bonaventure employs or implies almost all the kinship metaphors we have discussed, and, as is typical with imagery, they cannot be pressed without self-contradiction. It might seem that the odd image in this string of kinship titles is the architectural one: the mind is to be, along with daughter, spouse, friend, the 'house of God', a temple of the Holy Spirit. But Bonaventure is never far from Scripture, and here he follows Paul, who frequently places language of kinship and filiation in close proximity to imagery of the Temple as the supreme place of God's dwelling. In doing so, he stands well within Old Testament traditions of longing for future perfection, and probably echoes the teachings of Jesus himself.

Jesus reportedly compared his own body to the Temple. 'We heard him say', say his accusers, ' "I will destroy this

---

[3] Bonaventure, *The Soul's Journey into God*, trans. Ewert Cousins, Classics of Western Spirituality (New York: Paulist Press, 1978), 93.

Temple that is made with hands, and in three days I will build another, not made with hands"' (Mark 14: 58; cf. Matt. 26: 61, John 2: 19). John says he was speaking of his own body (John 2: 21). The Temple, since the establishment of Jerusalem by David and the building of its Temple by his son Solomon to house the Ark of the Covenant, was identified as the symbolic heart of God's presence with Israel. To identify Jesus with the Temple, whether Jesus himself did so or his followers, is to suggest that the body of Christ is now the dwelling of the living God.

Paul frequently takes up the theme of 'body as temple'. As in the Old Testament, it is the place of God's dwelling, but in Paul, the followers of Jesus, both individually and collectively, are this temple. At the same time it is the living body of Christ. 'You are God's building', he tells the Corinthians,

According to the grace of God given to me, like a skilled master builder I laid a foundation, and someone else is building on it. Each builder must choose with care how to build on it. For no one can lay any foundation other than the one that has been laid; that foundation is Jesus Christ. Now if anyone builds on the foundation with gold, silver, precious stones, wood, hay, straw—the work of each builder will become visible, for the Day will disclose it (1 Cor. 3: 10–13a).

A more precise identity for this 'building' is given a few verses later: 'Do you not know that you are God's temple [*naos*, or "sanctuary"] and that God's Spirit dwells in you?' (1 Cor. 3: 16).

While Paul's image here is collective, elsewhere he suggests that the faithful are, *each one*, to be a living stone: each one is distinct, but together form the great building whose foundation is Christ. They are the kin of Christ and members of one another. In 2 Corinthians the apostle asks, 'What agreement has the temple of God with idols? For we are the temple of the living God.' A catena of Old Testament citations unfolds this image of the living temple, linking it explicitly with kinship titles:

> ... as God said,
> 'I will live in them and walk among them,
> and I will be their God,
> and they shall be my people.
> ....
> And I will be your father,
> and you shall be my sons and daughters,
> says the Lord Almighty.'
>
> (2 Cor. 6: 16–18)[4]

The corporateness of the building does not diminish the distinctiveness and difference of the individual stones which build up the whole. It is these that make it the dazzling, iridescent

---

[4] Compare Jer. 31: 1; Ezek. 27: 37; Isa. 43: 6 and 52: 11; Hos. 1: 10. Murray J. Harris draws attention also to 2 Sam. 7: 11–16, with its promise of a special sonship to David's line. Harris writes that 'God promises to David a royal dynasty that will last forever, including a special father–son relationship to Solomon and successive Davidic kings (2 Sam. 7. 14). This unique divine–human relationship, first promised to David's offspring and later extended to include the whole nation (Jer. 31. 9, '"I am Israel's father, and Ephraim is my firstborn son"'), now finds its fulfilment, Paul asserts, in the filial relationship of the Christian community to God as Father' (Murray J. Harris, *The Second Epistle to the Corinthians*, The New International Greek Commentary (Grand Rapids, Mich.: Wm. B. Eerdmans Publishing Company, 2005), 510. It is a matter of long debate as to whether 2 Cor. 6: 14–7: 1 is of Paul's authorship. Harris in his exhaustive commentary on the Epistle argues that it is; see esp. pp. 14–25. Stephen Hulgren suggests that the passage has its origins in Palestinian Jewish Christianity. Stephen J. Hulgren, '2 Cor.1.14–7.1 and Rev. 21.3–8: Evidence for the Ephesian Redaction of 2 Corinthians', *New Testament Studies*, 49 (2003), 39–56. Either way, these overlapping symbols of incorporation into the life of God are anchored deeply in Jewish piety and the Old Testament itself.

form it will become.[5] 2 Cor. 6: 16–18 has evident affinities to one of the climactic images of the Book of Revelation:

And I saw the holy city, the new Jerusalem, coming down out of heaven from God, prepared as a bride adorned for her husband. And I heard a loud voice from the throne saying, 'See, the home of God is among mortals. He will dwell with them, and they shall be his peoples, and God himself will be with them; he will wipe every tear from their eyes. Death will be no more; mourning and crying and pain will be no more, for the first things have passed away' (Rev. 21: 2–4).

God here dwells amongst the people with the intimacy of the tabernacling God of the Exodus, or the indwelling of the Word made flesh of John's gospel—a new family of brothers and sisters.[6]

In the elusive eschatological language of the New Testament, this tabernacling of God with men and women is both now and not yet: a promise of the presence, love, and beauty of a God who desires to be one with humankind. It appears from Paul that our future is convivial and not solitary. The bonds of love and friendship we have with one another (often achieved through the chafing and trials of life) are not means to this end, but constitutive of it—love of God, love of neighbour, and, perhaps most difficult of all, love of self all being requisite to final bliss.

We may acknowledge that we are loved by God, but it is more difficult to accept that we will be made lovely; yet this too is implied by the bridal imagery of Revelation. The seventeenth-century Puritan clergyman Samuel Crossan spoke more boldly

[5] For the bejewelled Jerusalem, in Revelation made 'bride', see Rev. 21: 18–21. Compare Tob. 13: 16 and Isa. 54: 11–12.
[6] The Greek for 'dwell' in Rev. 21: 3, as in John 1: 14 is 'tabernacle'. Later in the same chapter, John of Patmos says that he saw 'no temple in the city, for its temple is the Lord God the Almighty and the Lamb' (21: 22).

of future promise in what are now the words of a familiar hymn, 'My Song is Love Unknown':

> My song is love unknown, my Saviour's love to me;
> Love to the loveless shown, that they might lovely be.

We shall not only be loved, but 'lovely be' through the kindness of God.

# Bibliography

Aelred of Rievaulx, *Spiritual Friendship*, ed. Mary E. Laker. Kalamazoo, Mich.: Cistercian Publications, 1977.

Altmann, Alexander, ' "Homo Imago Dei" in Jewish and Christian Theology', *Journal of Religion*, 38/3 (1968), 235–59.

Anderson, B. W., *Creation in the Old Testament*. Philadelphia: Fortress; London: SPCK.

Aquinas, St Thomas, *Summa Contra Gentiles*, Book IV: 'Salvation', trans. Charles J. O'Neil. London and Notre Dame, Ind.: Notre Dame University Press, 1975.

—— *Summa Theologiae*. London: Eyre & Spottiswoode, 1964.

Arendt, H., *The Human Condition*. Chicago and London: University of Chicago Press, 1998.

Athanasius, St, *Contra gentes* and *De Incarnatione*, ed. R. W. Thomson. Oxford: Clarendon Press, 1971.

—— *The Trinity*, trans. New York: New City Press [for the] Augustinian Heritage Institute, 1990.

Augustine, *City of God*, trans. Henry Bettenson (London: Penguin Classics, 1984).

—— *Confessions*. London: Hodder & Stoughton, 1997.

—— *The Literal Meaning of Genesis*, ed. John Hammond Taylor, SJ New York: Newman Press, 1982.

—— *On Christian Teaching (de doctrina Christiana)*, ed. R. P. H. Green. Oxford: Oxford University Press, 1997.

# Bibliography

AYRES, L., 'The Christological Context of Augustine's *de Trinitate* XIII: Toward Relocating Books VIII–XV', *Augustinian Studies*, 29 (1998), 111–39.

BAKER, DENISE, *Julian of Norwich's Showings: From Vision to Book*. Princeton: Princeton University Press, 1994.

BAKHTIN, M. M., *Problems of Dostoevsky's Poetics*, trans. R. W. Rotsel (Ann Arbor: Ardis, 1973).

BARR, J., 'The Image of God in the Book of Genesis: A Study of Terminology', *John Rylands University of Manchester Bulletin*, 51 (Autumn 1968).

—— 'Abba Isn't "Daddy"', *JTS* 39 (1988).

BARTH, KARL, *Church Dogmatics*, III. 1: *The Doctrine of Creation*, ed. G. W. Bromiley and T. F. Torrance. Edinburgh: T. & T. Clark, 1961.

BAUERSCHMIDT, F. C., *Julian of Norwich and the Mystical Body of Christ*. Notre Dame, Ind.: University of Notre Dame Press, 1999.

BERNARD OF CLAIRVAUX, *On the Song of Songs*, ii, trans. K.J. Walsh (Kalamazoo, Mich.: Cistercian Publications, 1983).

BOESAK, A. A., *Black and Reformed: Apartheid, Liberation and the Calvinist Tradition*, ed. L. Sweetman. Maryknoll, NY: Orbis Books, 1984.

BONAVENTURE, St, *The Soul's Journey into God*, trans. E. Cousins, Classics of Western Spirituality (New York: Paulist Press, 1978).

BRAGUE, R., trans. FAGAN, T. L., *The Wisdom of the World: The Human Experience of the Universe in Western Thought*. Chicago and London: University of Chicago Press, 2003.

BRAIDOTTI, ROSI, *Patterns of Dissonance: A Study of Women in Contemporary Philosophy*. Cambridge: Polity, 1991.

BRENNAN, T., *History after Lacan*. London and New York: Routledge, 1993.

BROCK, R. N., *Journeys by Heart: A Christology of Erotic Power*. New York: Crossroad, 1988.

# Bibliography

BUBER, M., *I and Thou: With a Postscript by the Author Added.* Edinburgh: T. & T. Clark, 1958.

—— *Between Man and Man*, trans. Ronald Gregor Smith, London: Kegan Paul, 1947.

—— and Rosenzweig, F., *Scripture and Translation*, trans. Lawrence Rosenwald with Everett Fox (Bloomington: Indiana University Press, 1994).

BUCKLEY, M. J., *At the Origins of Modern Atheism*. New Haven: Yale University Press, 1987.

BYNUM, C. W., *Fragmentation and Redemption: Essays on Gender and the Human Body in Medieval Religion*. New York: Zone Books, 1991.

CALVIN, J., *The Institutes. of Christian Religion*, ed. T. Lane and H. Osborne. London: Hodder & Stoughton, 1986.

CARR, A., *Transforming Grace: Christian Tradition and Women's Experience*. New York: Continuum, 1998.

CHOPP, R. S., *The Power to Speak: Feminism, Language, God*. New York: Crossroad, 1989.

CHRYSOSTOM, ST. JOHN, *Baptismal Instructions*, trans. P. W. Harkins. New York: Paulist Press, 1963.

CICERO, *Laelius on Friendship*, trans. W. A. Falconer, Loeb Classical Library, 20. Boston: Harvard University Press, 1923.

CLARK, E. (ed.), *Women in the Early Church*. Wilmington, Del.: Michael Glazier, 1983.

CLARK, J. P. H., 'Time and Eternity in Julian of Norwich', *Downside Review*, 109 (1991), 259–75.

CONGAR, Y., *I Believe in the Holy Spirit*. London: Chapman, 1983.

COUNTRYMAN, L. W., *Dirt, Greed, and Sex: Sexual Ethics in the New Testament and their Implications for Today*. Philadelphia: Fortress Press, 1988.

DALY, M., *Beyond God the Father*. Boston: Beacon Press, 1973.

DE BEAUVOIR, S. & *The Second Sex*, trans. and ed. H. M. Parshley. London: Pan, 1988.

# Bibliography

DE BEAUVOIR, S. *De Ecclesia: The Constitution of the Church of Vatican Council II*, ed. G. Baum and E. H. Peters. London: Darton, Longman & Todd, 1965.

DE GRUCHY, J., 'The Revitalization of Calvinism in South Africa: Some Reflections on Christian Belief, Theology, and Social Transformation', *Journal of Religious Ethics*, 14/1 (Spring 1986), 22–47.

DILLISTONE, F. W., and TILLICH, P., *Myth and Symbol*. London: SPCK, 1966.

EVANS, C. A., and SANDERS, J. A. (eds.), *Early Christian Interpretation of the Scriptures of Israel: Investigations and Proposals*. Sheffield: Sheffield Academic Press, 1997.

FIORENZA, E. S., COLLINS, M., and LEFÉBURE, M. (eds.), *Women: Invisible in Theology and Church*. Edinburgh: T. & T. Clark, 1985.

FRYMER-KENSKY, TIKVA, *Studies in Bible and Feminist Criticism*. Philadelphia: The Jewish Publication Society, 2006.

FURLONG, M., *Mirror to the Church: Reflections on Sexism*. London: SPCK, 1988.

—— *Gaudium et spes: Pastoral Constitution on the Church in the World of Today*. London: Catholic Truth Society, 1966.

GIBSON, J., 'Could Christ have been Born a Woman?', *Journal of Feminist Studies in Religion*, 8 (Spring 1982), 65–82.

GILSON, E., *The Spirit of Medieval Philosophy*. New York: Charles Scribners Sons, 1940.

GOETHE, J. W., *Farbenlehre*, ed. Gerhard Off and Heinrich O. Proskauer, 3 vols. Stultgart: Verlag Freies Geislesleben, 1979.

GOLDSTEIN, S., 'The Human Situation—A Feminine View', *Journal of Religion*, 40 (1960), 100–12.

GOUX, J-J., 'The Phallus: Masculine Identity and the "Exchange of Women"', *differences*, 4/1 (Spring 1992), 42–75.

GREGORY OF NYSSA, *Select Works*, Nicene and Post-Nicene, Fathers, 2nd ser., vol. v. Grand Rapids, Mich.: Wm. B. Eerdmans Publishing Company, 1979.

# Bibliography

GREY, M., 'The Core of our Desire: Re-Imaging the Trinity', *Theology*, 93 (1990), 363–72.

HADOT, P., *What is Ancient Philosophy?*, Cambridge, Mass., and London: Belknap Press of Harvard University Press, 2004.

HAMPSON, D., *Theology and Feminism*. Oxford: Basil Blackwell, 1990.

—— and Ruether, R. R., 'Is There a Place for Feminists in a Christian Church?'. *New Blackfriars*, 68 (1987), 7–24.

HARRIS, MURRAY J., *The Second Epistle to the Corinthians*, The New International Greek Commentary. Grand Rapids, Mich.: Wm. B. Eerdmans Publishing Company, 2005.

HARRISON, C., *Beauty and Revelation in the Thought of Saint Augustine*. Oxford: Clarendon Press, 1992.

HARRISON, V., 'Male and Female in Cappadocian Theology'. *Journal of Theological Studies*, 41 (1990), 441–71.

HARVEY, SUSAN, ASHBROOK, 'Feminine Imagery for the Divine: The Holy Spirit, the Odes of Solomon, and Early Syriac Tradition' *St Vladimir's Theological Quarterly*, 37/2–3 (1993), 111–39.

HAUKE, M., *Women in the Priesthood?: A Systematic Analysis in the Light of the Order of Creation and Redemption*. San Francisco: Ignatius Press, 1988.

HORWITZ, R., and BUBER, M., *Buber's Way to 'I and thou': An Historical Analysis and the First Publication of Martin Buber's Lectures 'Religion als Gegenwart'*. Heidelberg: Schneider, 1978.

HULGREN, STEPHEN J., '2 Cor.1.14–7.1 and Rev. 21.3–8: Evidence for the Ephesian Redaction of 2 Corinthians', *New Testament Studies*, 49 (2003), 39–56.

HUME, DAVID, *Dialogues Concerning Natural Religion*, ed. N. Kemp-Smith. Indianapolis: Bobbs-Merrill, 1947.

IRIGARAY, L., *Speculum of the Other Woman*. Ithaca, NY: Cornell University Press, 1985.

IRIGARAY, L., *This Sex which is not One*. Ithaca, NY: Cornell University Press, 1985.

# Bibliography

IRIGARAY, L., *Je, tu, nous: Toward a Culture of Difference*. New York and London: Routledge, 1993.

JANTZEN, GRACE M., *Foundation of Violence: Death and the Displacement of Beauty*. New York: Routledge, Taylor & Francis Group, 2004.

JARDINE, A. A., *Gynesis: Configurations of Woman and Modernity*. Ithaca, NY, and London: Cornell University Press, 1985.

JOHNSON, E. A., 'The Incomprehensibility of God and the Image of God Male and Female', *Theological Studies*, 45 (Spring 1984), 441–65.

—— *She Who Is: The Mystery of God in Feminist Theological Discourse*. New York: Crossroad, 1993.

JOY, MORNY, 'Levinas: Alterity, the Feminine, and Women', *Studies in Religion/ Sciences Religieuses*, 22/4 (1993), 463–85.

JULIAN OF NORWICH, *The Showings of Julian of Norwich*, ed. Denise N. Baker, Norton Critical Edition. New York: W. W. Norton & Company, 2005. Also ed. Edmund Colledge, OSA, and James Walsh, SJ, Classics of Western Spirituality. Mahwah, NJ: Paulist Press, 1978.

KASPER, W., *The God of Jesus Christ*. London: SCM, 1984.

KENNY, A. J. P., *Aristotle on the Perfect Life*. Oxford: Clarendon Press, 1992.

KRISTEVA, J., *Desire in Language: A Semiotic Approach to Literature and Art*, with an introduction by L. S. Roudiez. New York: Columbia University Press, 1980.

—— *In the Beginning Was Love: Psychoanalysis and Faith*. New York: Columbia University Press, 1987.

—— L. S. Roudiez, *Powers of Horror: An Essay on Abjection*, with an introduction by New York: Columbia University Press, 1982.

KUHSE, H., and SINGER, P., *Should the Baby Live? The Problem of Handicapped Infants*. Oxford: Oxford University Press, 1985.

# Bibliography

KURYLUK, E., *Veronica and her Cloth: History, Symbolism, and Structure of a 'True' Image*. Cambridge, Mass., and Oxford: Basil Blackwell, 1991.

LA CUGNA, C. M., *God for Us: The Trinity and Christian Life*. San Francisco: HarperSanFrancisco, 1991.

LASH, N., *Easter in Ordinary: Reflections on Human Experience and the Knowledge of God*. London: SCM Press Ltd., 1988.

LAWLESS, G., 'Augustine and Human Embodiment'. In *Collectanea Augustiniana* (Lonvain: Lenven University Press, 1990), 167–86.

LE DOEUFF, M., *Hipparchia's Choice: An Essay Concerning Women, Philosophy, Etc.* Oxford: Basil Blackwell, 1991.

LEWIS, C. S., *A Grief Observed*. London: Fount, 1961.

—— *The Four Loves.* (1960). London: Fount, 1998.

LOCK, C., 'Reviewing Bakhtin', *St Vladimir's Theological Quarterly*, 43/1(1999), 85–90.

LONERGAN, B. J. F., *A Third Collection: Papers by Bernard J. F. Lonergan*, ed. F. E. Crowe, New York. Paulist Press; London: G. Chapman, 1985.

LOUTH, A., *The Origins of the Christian Mystical Tradition: From Plato to Denys*. Oxford: Oxford University Press, 1981.

MCFAGUE, S., *Models of God: Theology for an Ecological, Nuclear Age*. Philadelphia: Fortress Press, 1987.

MCGINN, B., 'The Human Person as Image of God: Western Christianity'. In B. McGinn, and J. Meyendorff (eds.), *Christian Spirituality: Origins to the Twelfth Century* (New York: Crossroad; London: SCM, 1985), 312–30.

MADEC, G., 'Christus, scientia et sapientia nostra: le principe de cohérence de la doctrine augustinienne', *Recherches Augustiniennes*, 10 (1975), 77–85.

MARION, J.-L., *God without Being*. Chicago: University of Chicago Press, 1991.

MARKUS, R. A., '*Imago* and Similitude in Augustine', *Revue des Études Augustiniennes*, 10 (1964), 125–43.

# Bibliography

MEEKS, W. A., 'Image of the Androgyne: Some Uses of a Symbol in Earliest Christianity', *History of Religions*, 13 (Fall 1974), 165–208.

METZ, J. B., SCHILLEBEECKX, E., and LEFÉBURE, M. (eds.), *God as Father?* Edinburgh: T. & T. Clark; New York: Seabury Press, 1981.

MIHAILOVIC, A., *Corporeal Words: Mikhail Bakhtin's Theology of Discourse*. Evanston, Ill.: Northwestern University Press, 1997.

MILLER, H., *Sexus*. London: Calder & Boyars, 1969.

MILLETT, K., *Sexual Politics*. London: Virago, 1970.

MILTON, J., *Paradise Lost*, ed. J. Leonard. London and New York: Penguin Books, 2003.

MURDOCH, I., *The Sovereignty of Good*. London: Routledge Classics, 2001.

MURRAY, R. 'The Bible on God's World and Our Place in It', *The Month* 21 (1988), 798–803.

NUSSBAUM, MARTHA, *The Fragility of Goodness: Luck and Ethics in Greek Philosophy*. Cambridge: Cambridge University Press, 1986.

O'DONOVAN, O., *The Problem of Self-Love in St. Augustine*. New Haven and London: Yale University Press, 1980.

OKURE, T., 'The Significance Today of Jesus' Commission to Mary Magdalene', *International Review of Mission*, 81 (Apr. 1992), 177–88.

PATEMAN, C., and GROSS, E., *Feminist Challenges: Social and Political Theory*. London: Allen & Unwin, 1986.

PORTER, R., and Tomaselli, S., *The Dialectics of Friendship*. London and New York: Routledge, 1989.

RADCLIFFE, T., 'Christ in Hebrews: Cultic Irony', *New Blackfriars*, 68 (1987), 494–504.

RICOEUR, P., *The Conflict of Interpretations: Essays in Hermeneutics*, trans. D. Inde. Evanston, Ill.: Northwestern University Press, 1974.

ROSENZWEIG, F., and GLATZER, N. N., *Franz Rosenzweig: His Life and Thought*. Indianapolis, Ind., and Cambridge: Hackett, 1998.

RUDDICK, S., *Maternal Thinking: Towards a Politics of Peace*. London: The Women's Press, 1990.

# Bibliography

RUETHER, R. R., 'The Liberation of Christology from Patriarchy', *New Blackfriars*, 66 (1985), 324–35.

SANDERS, E. P., (1990) *Jewish Law from Jesus to the Mishnah: Five Studies.* London: SCM Press; Philadelphia: Trinity Press International, 1990.

—— *Judaism: Practice and Belief, 63 BCE–66 CE.* London: SCM, 1992.

SCHLEIERMACHER, F. *On Religion: Speeches to its Cultured Despisers,* trans. R. Crouter. Cambridge: Cambridge University Press, 1996.

SCHNEIDERS, SANDRA M., *Beyond Patching: Faith and Feminism in the Catholic Church.* New York: Paulist Press, 1991.

SCHÜSSLER FIORENZA, E., *In Memory of Her: A Feminist Theological Reconstruction of Christian Origins.* London: SCM Press, 1983.

SEN, AMARTYA, and NUESBAUM, MARTHA (eds.), *The Quality of Life.* Oxford: Oxford University Press, 1993.

SINGER, PETER, *Animal Liberation: A New Ethics for our Treatment of Animals.* London: Cape, 1976.

SOSKICE, J. M., *Metaphor and Religious Language.* Oxford: Oxford University Press, 1985.

——, ed. *After Eve.* Basingstoke: Marshal Pickering, 1990.

—— 'The Symbolics of Staying On'. In D. Hampson, (ed.), *Swallowing the Fishbone: Christian and Post-Christian Feminism.* (London: SPCK, 1996).

—— 'Incarnation, Speech and Sociality in Schleiermacher and Augustine', in M. M. Olivetti, (ed.), *Incarnation,* Proceedings of the Castelli Colloquium (Padua: Cedam, 1999), 565–76.

—— and Lipton, D. (eds.), *Feminism and Theology.* Oxford: Oxford University Press, 2003.

STILLINGFLEET, E., *A discourse concerning the idolatry practised in the church of Rome . . . in answer to some papers of a revolted Protestant.* London: Printed by Robert White for Henry Mortlock, 1672.

SUTCLIFFE, T. and MOORE, P. eds. *In vitro veritas—More Tracts for our Time: St Mary's Annual for 1984/5,* London, St Mary's, Bourne Street, 1984.

# Bibliography

TAYLOR, C., *Sources of the Self: The Making of the Modern Identity*. Cambridge: Cambridge University Press, 1989.

THEISSEN, G., *Miracle Stories of the Early Christian Tradition*. Edinburgh: T. & T. Clark, 1983.

THISTLETHWAITE, SUSAN, B., *Sex, Race, and God: Christian Feminism in Black and White*. New York: Crossroad, 1989.

TRIBLE, P., *Texts of Terror: Literary-Feminist Readings of Biblical Narratives*. Philadelphia: Fortress Press, 1984.

VOGT, KARI, ' "Becoming Male": One Aspect of Early Christian Anthropology', in E. S. Schüssler Fiorenza, M. Collins, *et al.* (eds.), *Women: Invisible in Theology and Church*, (Edinburgh: T. & T. Clark, 1985), 72–83; repr. in J. M. Soskice and D. Lipton (eds.), *Feminism and Theology* (Oxford: Oxford University Press, 2003), 49–61.

WEIL SIMONE *Waiting on God*. London: Routledge & Kegan Paul, 1951.

—— *Gravity and Grace*. London: Routledge & Kegan Paul, 1963.

WILLIAMS, A. N., Contemplation: 'Knowledge of God in Augustine's *de Trinitate*'. In James J. Buckley and David S. Yeago (eds.), *Knowing the Triune God: The Work of the Spirit in the Practices of the Church* (Grand Rapids, Mich., and Cambridge: W. B. Eerdmans, 2001), 121–46.

WILLIAMS, R., 'The Paradoxes of Self-Knowledge in Augustine's *De trinitate*'. In J. Lienhard, SJ, Earl Muller, SJ, and Roland Teske, SJ (eds.), *Augustine Presbyter Factus Sum* (New York: Peter Lang, 1993).

—— '*Sapientia* and the Trinity: Reflections on *De trinitate*'. In *Collectanea Augustiniana* (Louvain: Leuven University Press, 1990), 317–32.

WITTGENSTEIN, L. *The Blue and the Brown Books*. Oxford: Basil Blackwell, 1958.

—— *Tractatus logico-philosophicus*. London: Routledge & Kegan Paul, 1955.

WOOLF, V., *A Room of One's Own*. London: Penguin, 2002.

# Index

Abba 77, 81
Adam 35, 40, 42, 43, 47, 50, 63, 71, 85,
  87, 89, 103, 135, 136, 137, 143, 144,
  149, 154, 166, 168
adoption 76, 145, 182
Aelred of Rievaulx 158, 159, 162,
  166, 189
Aers, David 139
affection 15, 16, 21, 24–7, 31, 163, 164
Africa 90
Albert the Great 85, 184
Agape 159, 160
*Alter ego* 164–6, 172
Ambrose 21 n, 71, 133 n, 135,
  157, 165
*Amicitia* 160, 176
Androgyny 108
anger, angry 77, 143, 144, 153, 162
animal 9, 16, 26, 27, 28, 31, 38, 40, 49,
  59, 60, 63, 64, 98, 111, 168
Anselm 129 n
anthropomorphism 1–6, 38, 76, 78
anthropology, Christian 4, 7–34,
  35–51, 52–65, 125–56
anti-Judaism 92
*Apatheia* 137, 208
Aquinas 37, 60, 69, 100 n, 119,
  129 n, 139
Arendt, Hannah 22
Aristotle 28, 167
Art, artist 7, 33, 35, 40, 87, 96, 139

ascent 3, 136, 137, 149
Athanasius 84, 116
Atonement 144, 145
attention 7–9, 22, 25–7, 32, 105
Augustine 12, 17–21, 24, 32, 37, 38,
  41, 43–5, 53, 116, 125, 127–38, 143,
  147–9, 152–5, 158, 165, 179–80
Ayres, Lewis 130

Baker, Denise 131 n
Bakhtin, Mikhail 177–9, 180
Barr, James 77 n
Barth 38 n, 50, 61, 104, 123, 131,
  148, 190
beauty, beautiful 8, 9, 10, 16, 18,
  21, 22, 27, 31, 49, 102, 166, 168,
  172, 187
Bernard of Clairvaux 88, 183
birth 2, 6, 15, 30, 43, 50, 79, 82, 87–91,
  96, 98, 105, 110, 117–18, 131, 133,
  145, 147, 150–1, 182
blood 84, 86–98, 118, 125, 138,
  141, 146
body 10, 12, 15–18, 20, 23, 28–31, 33,
  37, 38, 45, 84, 87–9, 106, 126, 132–9,
  142, 143, 146, 148, 151, 153, 160,
  184, 185
Bonaventure 184
Brague, Remi 37 n
Braidotti, Rosi 122 n
bride 78, 88, 89, 115, 187

# Index

Brock, Rita Nakashima 86 n
brother 13, 5, 6, 21, 24, 51, 78, 83, 89,
    112, 123, 145, 150, 181, 187
Buber 61, 62, 167, 169–76, 179, 191
Bynum, Caroline Walker 97–9

'Cartesian' man 9–12, 106, 121–2
*Causa sui* 122
children 6, 13, 15–19, 21, 24, 25, 32,
    39, 76, 79, 84, 90, 98, 145, 146,
    182, 183
Children of God 6, 79, 90, 91, 98, 146
Christ as mother 84–97, 115, 126,
    125–56
Christology 4, 36, 39, 84, 86, 154, 191
Chrysostom 71, 89, 192
Cicero 157–62, 164, 166, 167, 176, 192
Clement of Alexandria 78 n, 218
Clothed, clothing 140, 142, 144
Coakley, Sarah 112, 113
Congar, Yves 112 n
contemplative 5, 13–15, 17, 134–5
covenant 75, 185
creating 142, 146, 147
creation 9, 12, 35–51, 52–65, 96,
    140–1, 142, 147
Cross 17, 84–99, 117, 118, 125–56

Daly, Mary 71, 73, 193
Darwin, Charles 54
De Beauvoir, Simone 100, 101, 123
Derrida, Jacques 3, 105
*De Trinitate* (Augustine) 38, 125–56
dialogue 55, 157–80
Dostoevsky, Fyodor 177–80
dualism 106, 109, 119

ecstasis 25, 117
Eden 35–51, 143, 168, 178
embryo 29, 30, 57
Emmaus 183
enjoyment (Augustine on) 19–20
*Enkrateia* 16, 18, 25
Eros 163, 164
eschatology 36, 77, 146, 176, 181–8

essentialism 104, 202
ethical, ethics 8, 9, 27, 56, 60,
    159, 179
Eve 40–3, 48, 63, 71, 87, 89, 103,
    135–7, 154, 166
evil 19, 39, 137, 141, 153
excess 105, 115, 116
existentialism 101, 170

Fall 45, 143, 144, 152
father, fatherhood 1–3, 5, 16, 19, 47,
    66–78, 80–3, 86, 89, 90, 109, 120,
    123, 124, 132, 141, 144, 145, 147,
    150, 153, 166, 182, 186
fecundity 51, 95, 115
female body 87, 133
feminist, feminism 3, 4, 46, 66, 67, 70,
    72, 73, 80, 81, 83, 86, 92, 101, 104,
    106–8, 110–12, 115, 121
Fiorenza 93, 193
Fonrobert, Charlotte 94–7
fragile, fragility 140, 141, 142, 167, 200
Freud, Sigmund 39, 74, 106, 109
friend, friendship 90, 121, 157–67,
    170, 171, 175, 176, 180, 184, 187
Frymer-Kensky, Tikva 38 n, 50 n

*Gaudium et Spes* 45–8
Genesis 38, 40–2, 44, 45, 49, 52, 60,
    61, 63, 71, 97, 115, 134, 136,
    138, 147
Gibson, J. 85
gift 12, 112, 122, 155
Gilson, Etienne 130 n
Goldstein, Valerie Saiving 31 n, 103,
    104, 194
Goethe 26–7
Good 7, 8, 11, 18, 21–2, 26, 36, 39,
    41, 42, 51, 69, 77, 86, 128, 136,
    137, 141–3, 154, 158, 159, 161,
    162, 166, 182
Goux, J-J. 108, 109, 194
grace 35, 65, 112, 136, 144, 145,
    148, 152, 155, 172, 176, 178,
    182, 185, 192

# Index

Gregory of Nyssa 14, 18, 21 n, 24, 45 n, 79 n, 113, 194
Grey, Mary 111 n
growth 6, 7–34, 131, 151, 181

Hadot, Pierre 9
Hamerton-Kelly, Robert 75, 77
Harrison, Carol 137 n
Harvey, Susan Ashbrook 114
helper 42, 43, 135
Hill, Edmund 132 n, 152
holiness 5, 22 n 96, 98
Horwitz, Rivka 173 n
'human nature' 36, 64, 148, 149

'I am who I am' 5, 18, 44, 46, 61, 69, 70, 75, 79, 81, 82–6, 88–98, 110, 112, 115, 121, 122, 138, 140, 145, 147, 152, 157, 181, 183, 184, 185
'I and Thou' 169, 173, 174, 191
Imago Dei 11–16, 35–51, 79, 115, 121, 125–56
innascibility 117
Incarnation 11, 134, 150, 154, 161
individualism 24
infanticide 58, 59
intentionality 28, 215
Irigaray, Luce 105–8

Jairus's daughter 93, 96
Johnson, Elizabeth 86 n
Joy, Morny 123 n
Julian of Norwich 115–16, 125–56, 190

Kasper, Walter 111, 120, 197
kin, kinship 1–6, 20, 26, 59, 76–81, 90–1, 125–56, 181, 185
'know thyself' 39
Kristeva, Julia 31 n, 97–106
Kuhse, Helga 58, 59, 60, 63, 198

Lacan, Jacques 105, 121, 191
Last Supper 90
La Cugna, Catherine 118 n

Lash, Nicholas 110 n
Last Things 181–8
Law 50, 61, 76, 91, 92, 96, 97, 103
Lawless, George 133 n, 137 n
Le Doeuff, Michelle 101 n, 106 n
Leonard, Graham 91 n
Levinas, Emmanuel 100, 104, 123, 196
Leviticus 98
Lewis, C. S. 162–6, 198
liturgy 3, 68, 72, 81
Logos 105, 108, 109, 110
Lombard, Peter 85, 129, 132 n
Lord and his Servant 143
Lord's Prayer 76
Louth, Andrew 39 n, 63, 136 n
love 1, 7, 8–9, 18–26, 31, 34, 47, 48–51, 61, 66, 72, 77–8, 98, 100, 112–16, 118, 125, 127, 131, 138–53, 156, 158–65, 167, 171–2, 181–3, 187–8

McGinn, Bernard 133
Madec, Goulven 154
Magdalene, Mary 89, 90, 183
Marion, J-L. 117, 122, 199
marriage 5, 14–16, 18, 19, 24, 51, 52, 175
Mary (Virgin) 71, 114, 139, 140, 150
matter, *mater-ial* 21, 61, 109
*mens* 132, 153
menstruation 91, 92, 221, 223
mercy and grace 144, 148
metaphysics 54, 109, 110, 119, 122, 123
milk 88, 89, 114
Millet, Kate 102–4
Milton, John 103
Moltmann, Jürgen 82–3
Moses 2, 76, 78, 157, 167, 174, 181
mothers/mothering 1–6, 7–34, 78, 82, 84–9, 108–9, 112, 114–16, 118, 125–56, 181

# Index

Marcus Aurelius 17 n
Murdoch, Iris 7–10, 22, 32
Murray, Robert 64 n
mysticism 7, 26

name 1, 6, 64, 66, 67, 75, 76, 78, 79,
    82, 90, 106, 109, 112, 113, 118, 123,
    128, 146, 160, 173, 174
necessities 21, 135, 143
necessity (Weil on) 28–9
neighbour (love of) 157–81
neoplatonism 17, 109, 149
'new creation' 64, 96, 147, 181
New Jerusalem 187
Nussbaum, Martha 27, 45 n

Odes of Solomon 114
Okure, Teresa 89, 90, 201
Other 61, 100–24, 157–80

Paul, Saint 39, 41 n, 44 n,
    134, 182
parents 13, 30, 31, 120, 164
particularity 86, 141, 165
perform 131, 155, 156
*Philia* 159, 160
Philo of Alexandria 71
polyphonic 178
praise, praising 14, 50, 62, 84, 103,
    126, 145, 168, 180, 182
prayer 7, 13, 24, 30, 50, 66, 70,
    74–6, 179
pregnancy 29, 43, 84–99,
    125–56
presence 170, 173, 174, 185, 187
protology 52–65, 146, 181–8

Rahner, Karl 89 n
'received spirituality' 12, 14, 21
reciprocity, reciprocal 31, 51, 72, 160,
    161, 172, 173
Resurrection 44, 45, 53, 84, 90, 117,
    118, 181
Reuther, Rosemary Radford 72, 217
Ricoeur, Paul 74–81, 89

Rosenzwieg, Franz 167, 173–5,
    179, 201
Ruddick, Sara 23, 31 n

'sanctity of life' 58, 60, 63
*sapientia* 135, 137, 138, 152,
    154, 199
Schleiermacher, Friedrich 50, 168
science 10, 11, 25, 26, 36, 41, 52–55,
    57, 64–5
*scientia* 135, 137, 138, 152, 154, 199
second birth 145, 146, 147
'sexed' texts 107
sexual difference 35–51, 100, 108,
    113, 124
Shekinah 173–4
Siena, Catherine of 88
Sinai 174
Singer, Peter 58, 59, 60, 63, 198
slave 21, 22, 68, 90, 164, 178
Song of Songs 183
soteriology 36, 103, 146
'speaking thinking' 167, 175
speech 3, 38, 50, 68, 69, 78, 167–80
spiritual exercises 155
subjectivity 11, 101, 105, 123, 177,
    179, 180
suffering 28, 29, 139, 149, 151
Syriac 112, 114, 115

Taylor, Charles 7, 10, 21, 121 n
teleological 36
Temple 93
Theissen, Gerd 93
thirst 152, 182
Thistlethwaite, Susan Brooks 81 n
travail, travails 125–56
traveller, travelling 32, 131, 151, 152,
    155, 183
Trinity 4, 5, 40, 49, 50, 83, 100–24,
    125–56, 161
'two natures' 149

union 17, 131, 133, 135, 152, 172
'unselving' 18, 25

# Index

Veronica  96, 97, 198
virginity  14, 18

Way  1, 141, 148, 151, 154
Weil, Simone  7, 28, 29, 63
Williams, A. N.  155, 204, 210 n, 232 n

Williams, Rowan  133 n
Wittgenstein  67, 168
woman with the haemorrhage  92, 95, 96
Word made flesh  141, 152, 179, 187